BEYOND BUDS

Beyond Buds: Marijuana Extracts—Hash, Vaping, Dabbing, Edibles & Medicines
by Ed Rosenthal with David Downs

Copyright © 2014 Ed Rosenthal
Published by Quick American
A Division of Quick Trading Co.
Piedmont, CA, USA

ISBN: 978-1-936807-23-9
eISBN: 978-1-936807-24-6

Printed in Canada
Third Printing

Editor and Project Director: Elizabeth Fitzer
Contributors: David Downs, William Dolphin
Cover Design: Jennifer Touli Voss
Photo Editors: Jennifer Touli Voss, Darcy Thompson

Cover Photography
Top: Mel Frank
Bottom left: Ed Rosenthal
Bottom right: Saucey Santos

Library of Congress Control Number: 2014909265

BEYOND BUDS

– MARIJUANA EXTRACTS –

Hash, Vaping, Dabbing, Edibles & Medicines

by Ed Rosenthal

with David Downs

Dedicated to the Shulgins—
Pioneers in mind exploration

ACKNOWLEDGMENTS

We would like to thank the following individuals for their contributions, help, and support: Addison DeMoura and Steep Hill Halent Lab; Rick Pfrommer and Harborside Health Center; Bubbleman; Elemental Wellness; @fobextractions; Will F.; Dave Hodges of A2C2; HopeNet's Steve and Cathy; James and Holly of West Valley Tinctures; Mila Jansen; Jesse of A-Bear Concentrates; JonPaul and Scott from Bhang Chocolate; Jane Klein; Kenny M.; Marisa Lagos; Mark G.; Mel Frank; Jon Mendoza; Nikka T of Essential Extracts; John Oram, PhD, Cofounder/Senior Scientist of CW Analytical Laboratories; POP Naturals; Ramona Rubin of docGreen's; Rumpelstiltskin Extracts (i.e., RumpWax); Keith Woody; Josh Wurzer, President of SC Laboratories; Jennifer Carson; Shelli Newhart, PhD; Nadim Sabella; and Jason Schulz.

Franklin's Tower

Some come to laugh their past away
Some come to make it just one more day
Whichever way your pleasure tends
If you plant ice you're gonna harvest wind
Roll away the dew
Roll away the dew
Roll away the dew
Roll away the dew!!!!

—Robert Hunter
Courtesy of the Grateful Dead

Contents

Chem 91 Shatter.

Photo: Nadim Sabella Photography

Introduction

This book is about the world of marijuana beyond the bud.

The smoked bud can be helpful medically or a pleasant event. But it is only one way to experience the wonders that cannabis offers. This book is a guide to the many ways to prepare and use cannabis, beyond buds.

The quest for concentrates and their growing popularity is a return in part to pre-prohibition tradition, when cannabis was mostly ingested rather than smoked. Smoking is largely an artifact of prohibition. Before marijuana became illegal it was available in tinctures, pills, salves, and drinks, and one of its concentrates, hashish, was eaten. Without processed marijuana, users moved to inhalation only when other means of ingestion were unavailable. Now that prohibition is ending, aficionados and patients are returning to traditional methods of use and finding new ways of ingesting it.

For gardeners and farmers concentrates offer a solution to a conundrum they face. Parts of the plant contain THC but are not suitable for smoking. It makes sense to salvage these cannabinoids from the leaf and trim and tiny nugs, which comprise one-quarter to one-eighth the weight of the yield. To use, it just has to be collected. The collection and processing of this material is the subject of this book.

This is a great book if you are interested in alternatives to smoking bud, whether for medical or recreational use. It is a guide to both making and using these new marijuana products. It will provide you with some of the easiest and safest ways to make concentrates such as oils, waxes, budders, and shatter, as well as edibles, tinctures, and external preparations.

THE HISTORY OF THIS BOOK

Leaf products used to be called "trash" and were given away to cannabis-poor friends for baking or smoking. The moniker was not the result of low potency. Mexican marijuana often contains similar THC levels. The problem is the taste and harshness of the smoke, which is rough and acrid, with a high level of burning vegetation that hides aroma and taste. No one has a method of converting leaf into sweet bud; instead, the techniques described in this book separate cannabinoid-bearing glands from the rest of the vegetation. Glands are the only potent part of the plant, so after they are removed, the vegetation can be discarded.

The idea for my first book on using marijuana leaf/trim/small nugs, *Ask Ed: Marijuana Gold—Trash to Stash*, sifted through my mind for many years.

In 1979 the "Tilt Pipe," a sophisticated globe-type vaporizer, a precursor to the "Volcano," was released. With this device, you could use the low-quality pot generally available at the time and just inhale the essence. It made quite a difference. Unfortunately, the venture was doomed to failure because the War on Drugs was ramping up. Paraphernalia was outlawed, and since the Tilt had no other use than vaporizing pot, and because it had no "redemptive value" such as for use with tobacco, it became illegal.

In 1987 the late John Gallardi released his "Master Sifter." This device used vibration to knock the glands from grass. It was the first commercial unit available for the purpose. He also made a rolling tray/sifter with a stainless steel mesh surface and a sliding glass gland collector. I still use one of these as a rolling tray.

About the same time John was working on his trays, Nevil Schumacher of the Seed Bank showed me a piece of "water hash" he had made with Rob Clarke. It was an amazingly hard ball. Nevil chipped a piece off of the brittle material. When he lit it in a pipe, it melted and bubbled. He told me they had made the amazingly potent ball from leaf and trim using a water process.

Then, in the nineties, Mila Jansen, located in Holland, invented the Pollinator, and the bags for making water hash. These two devices and their imitators changed the way quantities of leaf and trim could be processed. The other development was the ongoing legalization of medical marijuana and devices for its use in states all over the country.

In 2002 I finally got around to writing *Ask Ed: Marijuana Gold—Trash to Stash*. This book helped to change peoples' attitude toward leaf/trim/small nugs and paved the way for the revolution that is still taking place regarding concentrates in the industry today.

Beyond Buds updates the techniques described in *Trash to Stash*, and details techniques for the new concentrates that have become popular.

Tahoe OG Kush.

Photo: Steep Hill Halent

Chapter 1.

Breaking Bud—

Selecting and Collecting Material

Leaves and trim, by-products of bud production, present an interesting paradox. At 5% to 20% THC, the bud is the plant's crown jewel, the gardener's reward for attentive caretaking. But cannabis produces THC on the leaves as well as the buds.

Small, bulbous, droplet-shaped, THC-containing resin glands coat the leaves and bracts, creating a natural protective barrier against insects, disease, herbivores, and the sun's UV rays. These glands contain one-quarter to one-eighth of the THC found in the buds. Fan leaves have a THC content of only 1% to 3%, so they are a poor smoking material. Trim, with a modest 2% to 6% THC content, commands only a little more respect than the leaves.

Original Grand Daddy Purple.

Photo: Steep HIll Halent

Buds typically weigh three to four times that of the leaf/trim/nugs with tremendous variation depending on variety and gardening technique. Still, the trim and fan leaves contain 10% to 20% of the plant's total THC production. In the past gardeners were often content to toss this material or give it to grass-poor friends rather than trying to extract the THC.

Today processing the leaf and trim for use as kief, hash, tincture, or other concentrates, or using it to make butter or other edibles, is part of the weed economy. Collecting leaves and trim doesn't add complexity to the harvest. Leaves are already being trimmed and bagged; trim from manicuring must already be managed. Being prepared to dry and store this material in advance makes the collection almost as simple as bagging it for the trash can. Once the leaf is saved for use, it only needs to be stored properly before transforming the material.

New inventions and techniques make it easy to process this secondary material. *Beyond Buds* offers traditional methods and recent innovations for

THE HIERARCHY OF BY-PRODUCT

Starting material is categorized according to its THC content:

1. Bud bits and pieces, or cosmetically challenged "popcorn bud"

2. Bag shake—the residue at the bottom of the bag

3. Primary trim—the small leaves near the bud sites

4. Mature fan leaves—the large sun leaves

5. Immature buds—these vary in THC content depending on stage of maturity

6. Immature trim/immature leaf—also variable depending on stage of development

7. Vegetative leaf—leaf from a plant that has not entered the flowering phase of growth; has the lowest THC content

Decreasing labor and expense during harvest is easy with the durable, high-speed Twister T4 auto trimmer. It's light weight and portable so you can take it into your garden, as well as easy to clean up.

Photo: Keirton Inc.

processing leaf and trim into worthwhile stash. A little information combined with the right tools maximizes the harvest and creates new ways to use it.

SELECTING AND COLLECTING MATERIAL

When tossing it out, trash is everything that isn't bud. Saving material to transform it requires a more discerning eye. Stems and woody parts of the plant are not useable since they contain few cannabinoids.

The quality of the remaining material is based on the percentage of THC it contains. Tetrahydrocannibinol (THC), the main psychoactive component of marijuana, as well as other cannabinoids, such as CBD and CBG, that give each variety a characteristic medical effect or high, are produced on the leaves surrounding the flowers, and stored in glands that protrude from the leaf surface.

GRADES OF LEAF

The flower areas of the female plant and the small leaves surrounding them contain the most THC—from twice to five times as much as the trim leaves. The fan leaves contain one-half to one-third the amount of cannabinoids as the trim leaves. Even so, the cannabinoids contained in these leaves are refinable.

Male plants also contain cannabinoids. They are strongest at the budding but pre-flowering stage. The small leaves near the flowers are the most potent, followed by the younger and then older fan leaves.

Use a magnifying glass or photographer's loupe for a close-up look at the material. The fan leaf glands are often small and hug the surface of the leaf, while the glands near the flowers are stalked and look like mushrooms with bulbous caps. The latter contain considerably more cannabinoids than the smaller glands.

Leaf with visible glands is worth keeping. Leaf from immature plants usually has very few glands and will not yield much. In a recycling effort, you may opt to trash material with the sparsest glands, such as the large fan leaves, while saving the smaller leaves, trim, and bud bits for use.

GLANDS AND QUALITY

The THC, CBD, and other cannabinoids are contained in the glands, but not all glands are created equal. Glands vary for several reasons, notably growing technique and genetics.

- The glands of some varieties are bigger than others. Larger glands hold more resin.

- Strains vary in density of glands.

- Some varieties have large numbers of smaller glands that carpet the plant.

- Some varieties grow more leaf than others. This results in more gland-bearing leaf and trim to transform.

- Resin quality varies by strain and cultivation methods. The quality of the resin affects the quality of the product. If the starting material—that is, the resin in the glands—is not very potent, concentrating it results in mediocre concentrate. Lower-potency material results in lower-quality product than high-quality material.

Sophisticated growers often keep the leaf separated by variety, just as they do with their buds. The quality of high associated with inhaling different varieties carries over to other methods of ingestion.

It is best to separate the trash into two rough categories of higher and lower quality. Separate large fan leaves from the higher potency trim. Also sort the popcorn bud, which has the most glands and will yield the most.

The material most suitable for each method is noted throughout the book. For instance, vaporizers can utilize high-grade bud bits or popcorn bud, but not leaf. However, leaf is suitable for making tinctures.

STORING THE GREEN

After the leaf is collected, dry it until crisp. It is important for the material to dry thoroughly because the molecule THCA is inactive as it occurs in the plant. It has a carbonate molecule (COOH) attached. When the plant dries out, the THC and other cannabinoids release the molecule. Chemically, THC acid becomes the psychoactive molecule THC.

You have a choice of methods for drying. Some people lay the material out flat on newspaper or screens on shelves and wait for it to dry, then bag it in plastic storage bags. If dealing with large quantities, or in particularly humid areas, run a fan and a dehumidifier in the drying area, for faster processing and to assure crispness, indicating low moisture. An electric food dehydrator set on low heat can speed or complete the drying process, but as the temperature rises more volatile terpenes evaporate.

Cannabinoids are destroyed in the presence of light and heat, especially around oxygen. The best possible way to preserve cannabis is to store it in the dark at a cool to cold temperature in an oxygen-free environment such as nitrogen or CO_2. It will keep for long periods when it is stored in sealed, opaque containers in a refrigerator.

Sealed, refrigerated, dried marijuana can be kept for several years with little deterioration.

In areas with high humidity, moisture will permeate any unsealed packaging and get into the material after it has dried. Should the moisture get too high the material is subject to attack by bacteria and mold. Rot is indicated by an ammonia odor. Mold develops as gray or white growth on the leaves. In either case, the material is ruined.

TIPS AND TRICKS—
THE ALCHEMY OF MARIJUANA PROCESSING

There are a few common rules to processing marijuana that will be mentioned throughout. These simple principles about the chemical nature and limits of marijuana are important for understanding how to process the plant material to result in a quality product.

Solubility

THC is not water soluble; it is soluble in oils, fats, and alcohol. The tinctures and foods presented in the book are extracts of THC from trim or leaves using alcohol, butter, or oil as the solvent.

Assimilation

Assimilation refers to the time it takes for cannabis to have an effect after it is used. Another aspect of assimilation is the quantity that is required to reach a certain state of medication or highness. Different methods of intake are assimilated with varied efficiency. Smoking, vaporizing, tinctures, and eating all produce distinct highs.

The benefit of quick assimilation is that it is easier to titrate, to figure out how much to use. Smoking or vaporizing has a fast onset, so you know quickly whether or not you have a sufficient dose.

Ingesting tinctures sublingually—that is, droplets placed under the tongue—is almost as fast as smoking or vaporizing, because it goes directly into the bloodstream from the mucous membranes, the same way smoke is absorbed by the blood in the lungs. Five minutes after a tincture is dropped on the tongue, its effects are felt.

Drinking or eating cannabis has a slower onset. One important factor is whether cannabinized food is eaten on an empty or full stomach. Food is digested more efficiently and faster on an empty stomach; the high starts coming on after 20 to 30 minutes and peaks in one or two hours. It can be intense with several peaks and last four hours or more, but it is more likely to last two to three. On a full stomach, the high begins 45 to 60 minutes after ingestion and peaks two to three hours later. It may last four or five hours or more, but it is not as intense.

While the high can be enjoyable and long lasting, it is harder to determine the right amount to use since the feedback loop can take up to four hours. As a result it is easier to eat more or less than intended and end up with a too-heady buzz, or not much of a buzz at all.

Dosage

Assimilation differs from person to person and is not entirely attributable to a person's weight or metabolism. Other factors may make what is not enough for one person too much for another.

Trying to distinguish between marijuana's psychoactive and therapeutic effects is difficult. It is also difficult to establish a consistent dosage through all methods of intake. When the same material is used and the same processes are followed, this is somewhat easier to determine. Caution should always be used when trying out a new variety or a new technique for processing. It may take a little careful experimentation to find the right amount, and the amount that is right for you may not be the same for someone else.

Kief.

Photo: Steep Hill Halent

Chapter 2.

Kief/ Dry Sift—

Manual, Machine, Dry Ice

Kief, also known as "Dry Sift," is composed of the unpressed glands scraped from dried mature flowers and leaves using a screen. It is very popular because it is easily gleaned from leaves and trim.

Kief is the easiest marijuana product you can make. Tiny resin-filled glands cover the buds and leaves. These tiny stalked glands, known as trichomes, are the only part of the plant that contain significant amounts of cannabinoids, such as THC and CBD, as well as the pungent terpenes that give each

Dry Sift.

Photo: Ed Rosenthal

marijuana strain its distinctive aroma, taste, and medical and psychoactive qualities. Making kief consists of collecting those trichomes. There are a number of techniques for separating them from the plant material and sorting them.

Celebration Pipe's large bowl is perfect for smoking with friends—try some kief on a bed of bud. Made from lava stoneware, the pipes are individually sculpted, then plated with precious metals.

Kief can be smoked just as it is collected; you can add the kief to your pipe without further processing or preparation. It is often pressed to make hash. It can also be used to produce tinctures or cooking ingredients. Those uses are discussed in their respective chapters. This chapter explains various screening techniques to produce kief, as well as two methods using dry ice to enhance the process.

Because kief is so easy to collect from dried cannabis, it is one of the oldest marijuana preparations and is known in many corners of the world. Alternately spelled as *kif, kief, kef,* or *kiff,* the word appears in many languages. The origin of the word is the Arabic *kayf,* which means well-being or pleasure. The term was historically used in Morocco and elsewhere to mean a mixture of marijuana and tobacco, not unlike modern-day blunts, though it was typically smoked using hookahs. In Amsterdam and other parts of Europe, kief is sometimes called *pollen* or *polm,* and many of the screens and devices used to separate kief from other plant material are called pollen screens or pollen sifters.

The marijuana plant produces three basic types of resin-rich glands that grow to different sizes expressed in microns or micrometers, which is a metric measurement equal to one millionth of a meter. Marijuana glands or trichomes range from as small as 15 microns to as large as 500 microns. That lets you easily separate the different glands by using screens of corresponding sizes.

The bulbous glands are the smallest, ranging from 10–15 microns. These tiniest glands perch atop equally tiny one-cell stalks that cover the leaves of late vegetative plants.

The capitate-sessile glands are the middle size, ranging from 25–100 microns, and are more numerous than the bulbous glands. "Capitate" means globular, and that's what they look like—spherical globs of resin that lay on the leaf and flower surfaces.

Capitate-stalked glands are the ones most visible on the buds of mature, flowering marijuana plants, as these rich resin balls are the largest at 150–500 microns, and they sit high on stalks that can reach 500 microns. These are the glands that hold most of the cannabinoids and terpenes and are found most abundantly on the upper leaves, flowers, and bracts (the tiny leaves surrounding the flowers) of unfertilized female plants. These are the glands that are captured to make kief.

Some grinders come with an extra compartment that catches kief.

Photo: Wacky Willy's

The maturity of the plant and its variety and environmental conditions all affect gland size. For instance, many Moroccan varieties may have glands that are under 80 microns. Many sativa varieties also have small glands. "Hash plant" varieties often have glands that are 120 microns or larger. Most sinsemilla is in the mid-range, between 80–110 microns.

To give you a sense of these sizes, a human hair is about 70 microns or a bit more; the finest beach sand is 100 microns; playground sand is roughly 250 microns; and the eye of a needle is more than 1200 microns.

To measure the size of the glands with precision in the marijuana you're working with, use a microscope and a slide with a micron scale etched on it. Some microscopes come equipped with a scale called a reticule built into one of the eyepieces to measure microns. Count the number of hash marks the gland spans and multiply by the conversion factor for the magnification power.

HOW KIEF SCREENING WORKS

THC and other cannabinoids and terpenes are concentrated in glands that cover many parts of the marijuana plant, but they are concentered in the upper leaves, flowers, and flower bracts of unfertilized female plants. They are also found on the seed covering and surrounding areas of pollinated plants. Screening cured plant material is one of the easiest ways to rescue these glands for use.

There are several different methods to prepare the plant material for processing and for screening or sifting kief. In countries close to the 30th parallel, such as Nepal, Afghanistan, and Lebanon, small amounts of kief have traditionally been made using a silk scarf stretched tightly over a bowl. Dried marijuana, frequently cured for as much as six months, is rubbed on the taut silk cloth. The cloth's fine weave allows the small glands to pass through to the bowl, leaving the vegetative material on top. Silk scarves are still used in parts of the world, but the nylon or metal mesh screens used for printing (still often called silk screens) are more durable and come in a variety of dimensions and mesh sizes.

One of the simplest methods of making kief is by gently rubbing the plant material over a fine screen. The size of the open-

Assortment of Dry Sift and Bubble Hash.

Photo: Ed Rosenthal

ings in the screen determines which size glands and how much residual plant material will make it through. The vigor used in rubbing it on the screen has a profound effect on the quality of the final product. Different grades of kief are produced by varying the amount of time the material is sifted, the screen's gauge, and the pressure used. Sifting the same material a few times yields more kief, but each sift results in a higher proportion of plant mixed with the glands. Kief color ranges from golden-white for the purest kief to a greenish gold. The greener it is, the more plant material it contains.

Kief or pollen-sifting boxes are good tools for making small amounts. They can be as simple as wooden stash boxes with a screen above a pullout drawer that catches the glands that fall off your weed in normal handling. Other boxes are made specifically to capture different grades of kief, separating the glands from the vegetation by shaking it. Over-vigorous shaking or rubbing is counterproductive because too much vegetation is collected, lowering the quality. Use cold material. Freezing makes it crisp so the glands break free easier.

Some larger sifters are automated much like a paint mixer, so you can add the material, flip a switch, and let the sifter do the work.

Compact DIY solutions are inexpensive and easy to make using screens used for printing T-shirts and posters. All you need is the proper screen, a frame to stretch it on, and a smooth hard surface such as glass or metal to collect the kief.

Printing screens made of nylon, polyester, or metal are available at art supply stores or online. The mesh sizes are typically described in terms of the number of threads per inch, so a higher number is a finer screen. Meshes range from around 40 to 400, with 110 and 156 being the most common for printing T-shirts. Screen mesh from fine to coarse can be purchased pre-stretched in aluminum or wood frames, or as rolls or sheets.

PREPARING FOR SCREENING

Very little preparation or work is needed to make excellent kief. Kief making is so quick that small quantities can be sifted or sieved easily while trimming cured bud or preparing for another process.

Thoroughly clean the material by removing seeds, stems, and sticks.

Photo: David Downs

Kief is best made from dry, well-cured, coarse marijuana. Many people like to salvage kief from trim that they might otherwise discard. The stems can be sorted out, but don't have to be. The more bud bits you use, the better quality kief you'll get.

For the best results, start with trim and leaf that is dry but not overly crisp. If it is too dry the vegetative material becomes brittle and can crumble into dust or powder that can pass through the screen along with the glands you're trying to collect. Kief made from over-dried material contains more green matter, tastes more like chlorophyll, and is less potent. Similarly, densely pressed material or "brick" marijuana does not work as well for kief as loose material does.

When to Sieve

In the mountains of the Hindu Kush region, hash makers have traditionally waited for cold, dry weather to sift their kief. Curing is key to all fine marijuana products, so waiting for the cold is a way of making sure that the buds drying in open air are in a state of prime readiness. Cold also freezes the dry leaves and trim, making the tiny trichome stalks brittle. That lets the glands break free more easily. Less agitation or pressure to free the glands results in less vegetative material in the kief. As a practical benefit, keeping the glands intact also reduces the amount of resin clogging the screen, though this rarely happens, even in moderate temperatures.

As with overly dry marijuana, overly brittle, frozen vegetative material can become powder and pass through the screen. Moistening the material by airing it in a space with high humidity might help. Using a finer screen may be another solution. Having several sizes of screen mesh allows you to use the right one for the material and temperature.

To make pro-quality kief, the colder the plant material you start with, the better. Prepare the material by putting it in a freezer overnight.

There is no need to overthink the process. Remember, kief is simple. Kief of decent quality can be made in all weather conditions. Cool temperatures, around 60°F (15°C) or lower, are best for working with marijuana. Low to moderate humidity is okay, and if the material is particularly dry, a little extra humidity can be helpful.

MANUAL SCREENING

Manual screening is cost effective and no more labor intensive than sifting flour. It is possible to buy ready-made screens or kief boxes from many sources and in many sizes. The screen, usually wire mesh, comes framed and often includes a solid bottom drawer where the kief is collected. Most art supply stores sell plastic screens for printing that are already stretched on frames made of wood or aluminum.

Making your own screens or boxes requires no special skill. Frames to stretch screens over are

Turning any chair into a comfortable workstation, the Trim Bin from HarvestMore reduces stress injuries and increases productivity. The tray includes a screen to catch glands.

GLANDS AND SCREENS: A GUIDE

Matching screen size to gland size is important for maximizing your kief yield.

Most marijuana glands are typically between 75–125 microns or micrometers, though they vary based on the type of gland, the maturity of the plant, and other factors.

Mesh screens are usually sized by a "mesh" measurement that indicates how many strands of wire or nylon it has for every inch of material. Detailed mesh-to-micron conversion charts can be found online, but the chart below shows common mesh sizes and the micron size of the openings between strands. (LPI stands for lines per inch.)

Kief sifting generally works best with screens between 100 and 130 microns. Plants with larger crystals need a screen of 150 microns to capture the glands. Screens in the range of 100–150 lines per inch usually work well. But not all mesh sizes are created equal. The size of the openings varies based on the diameter of the strands. Screens made of nylon, polyester, or stainless steel have different strand diameters at any particular mesh size, and finer mesh screens use strands of smaller diameters. Stainless steel screens are the most durable and don't shed. Plastic and nylon screens should be replaced periodically because they shed strands as they age and wear.

Inches	LPI	Microns	Millimeters
0.0021	270	53	0.053
0.0024	230	63	0.063
0.0029	200	74	0.074
0.0035	170	88	0.088
0.0041	140	105	0.105
0.0049	120	125	0.125
0.0059	100	149	0.149
0.0070	80	177	0.177

easy to make or buy. Just decide how big you want it, and pick a screen size and material. Stainless steel mesh screen or "wire cloth" is sturdy, durable, and rarely needs cleaning. Nylon or polyester silk screen mesh is more flexible but should be replaced annually. The frames and silk screen materials are available at art supply stores.

If you build your own screen or have a screen without a tray, a piece of glass or mirror makes a good surface for catching the kief and gathering it up. Whatever you use, smoothness is the crucial quality of a catch tray, as the glands you're collecting can be smaller than the diameter of a human hair. You don't want to lose any to texture. A credit card, ID, business card, or other straight edge can be used to gather the filtered material into a pile.

THE SCREENING PROCESS

Place the collection tray under the screen. Start with a handful of trim, leaf, or small nugs, as you prefer. Leaf doesn't require any preparation before rubbing but use a grinder to prepare the bud.

Once you've ground the bud, or if using the whole leaves, gently rub the material softly against the screen. A softer touch or action minimizes the amount of vegetative matter that passes through and keeps more of the glands intact. This first pass is the cleanest and most potent kief.

Connoisseurs sometimes use multiple screens progressing from coarser to finer mesh. In the first pass, they use a mesh with fewer than 100 strands per inch. This first screening cleans out the bulk of the vegetative matter. The sifted material is collected and placed on a finer-mesh screen. Since the material has already been reduced to a coarse grind by the first screen, the second, finer

SCREEN RESOURCES

Ace Screen Supply Company
AceScreenSupply.com

Dick Blick Art Materials
DickBlick.com

Howard Wire Cloth Co.
HowardWire.com

Jo-Ann Fabrics
Joann.com

Ryonet
Ryonet.com

MAKING YOUR OWN SCREEN

Equipment

- Thick wooden picture frame, or a frame constructed of wood at least 1" x 1"
- Wire cloth or silk screen mesh cut large enough to wrap around to the underside of the frame
- $3/8$" wire tacks or staple gun

Cut the wire cloth or mesh to fit over the frame with an inch or more to spare on each side, depending on the thickness of the frame—the screen should wrap around the sides of the frame. For instance, if the wood frame is 15" x 6", cut the wire cloth to 17" x 8", which leaves an extra inch on each side.

Stretch the screen taut and fasten it securely using tacks or staples on one side, then pull it tight and secure the opposite end to the other side of the frame. Repeat with the other two sides.

Screens of varying micron grades from Fresh Headies.

100 lpi - 160 micron
120 lpi - 140 micron
140 lpi - 107 micron
200 lpi - 70 micron

screen only needs to be shaken or tapped lightly to create cleaner kief. The kief remaining on the second screen should be saved—for ingestion, capsules, tinctures, or salves. Screening with successively finer meshes yields different products and flavors.

Keep the first sift light and brief, up to a minute. This yields the finest grade of kief, but the yield is fairly low. The biggest, most mature glands are the first to break free and sift through. Only the first few minutes of screened material is pleasant smoking material. The yield from the second sift is still potent but of considerably lower quality than the first. It is greener and has more of a taste of chlorophyll. After the first two sifts the material can be screened a third time for as long as 10 minutes, and the resulting product can be used for ingestion or external purposes, or for further purification.

When screening by hand a soft touch and proper screen are important, as is maintaining the right environmental conditions. Experimentation is easy, low cost, and fun, so even the complete novice can figure out how to create top-quality kief with minimal fuss.

Even if it is not your preferred product, kief is so cheap and easy to screen in small amounts that everyone should try it. For those who appreciate its pure flavor or other uses enough to focus on producing larger quantities, a drum machine or industrial sifter may be a worthwhile investment. There are many kief sieves available, often marketed as pollen sifters.

MACHINE SCREENING

If you have a lot of leaf and trim that you'd like to process for kief, you may soon find manual screening to be tiresome and inefficient. You'd not be the first. For high-volume kief making, simple drum machines automate much of the task. As a bonus, they typically gather a higher percentage of glands from the plant material than flat screening by hand.

The Pollinator

The Pollinator is the original drum machine developed by Mila Jansen, a hash aficionado from the Netherlands who lived for years in the Hindu Kush region. Mila spent her fair share of time manually screening kief in cold weather. Luckily for the rest of us, Mila is an innovator.

One evening after a long, tedious day of screening, Mila was home doing laundry when the clothes dryer caught her attention. In a flash, she realized that the dryer was essentially doing the same thing she had been doing all day! Soon thereafter, she invented an electric-powered tumbler for her personal use. It would be a few years before it occurred to her that this machine might be marketable, but when it did, the Pollinator was the result.

The Pollinator is available in a few sizes to accommodate different needs. You just place the material to process inside and turn it on. The machine

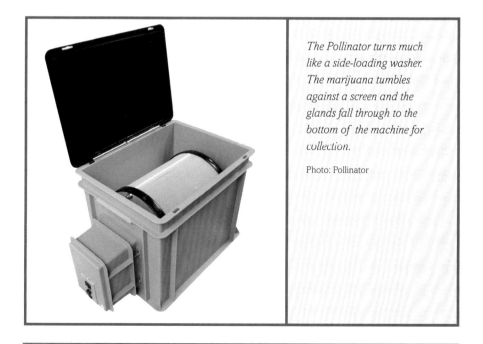

The Pollinator turns much like a side-loading washer. The marijuana tumbles against a screen and the glands fall through to the bottom of the machine for collection.

Photo: Pollinator

tosses it softly against a fine screen, around 130 strands per inch. The amount of time it runs determines the quality of the kief collected. Presses and water hash equipment (like the Ice-O-Lator) are also available through the Pollinator Company.

DRY ICE KIEF—THE MANUAL METHOD

Perhaps the cheapest, simplest way to concentrate cannabinoids is also one of the newest. Since 2009, hash makers have been turning to dry ice—which is frozen carbon dioxide—to yield an impressive amount of kief. Dry ice is the fastest way to turn trash into gold. Manual dry ice sieving is very inexpensive to set up, results in very little mess or cleanup, and doesn't involve explosive chemicals like BHO, or require expensive machinery.

One-Minute Dry Ice Kief is my favorite concentrate. It is very smooth and contains a lot of terpenes because it is made cold and not mixed with anything, even water, preserving the terpenes. It has very little vegetation so you are inhaling only gland products.

Equipment

- Cannabis (1 ounce, dry trim or fresh-frozen)
- Bubble Bags (durable 160- and 220-micron water bubble bags)
- 5-gallon bucket
- Clean, sanitary surface area—at least four feet long
- Collection tool (such as a plastic scraper)
- Dry ice—3 pounds, broken up into small pieces

Method

Manual dry ice sieving uses the -106°F (-76°C) temperature of dry ice to freeze the waxy stalks of the trichomes, making them brittle enough to mechanically snap off during agitation. The snapped glands then fall through the 160- or 220-micron bag onto a surface and get collected.

First, designate a clean, sanitary, indoor space with a table with a clean surface. Sanitary conditions are important. You don't want to find dog hair or other contaminants in the final product. Set up a large table in the clean room, and cover it with some parchment paper.

Place trim or ground bud in the bucket. Add dry ice. Tightly affix the 160-micron bubble bag over the top of the bucket using large rubber bands so that when you eventually turn the bucket upside down, the dry ice and trim fall onto the screen.

Pick up the bucket and gently shake to help distribute the cold. After a minute, turn the bucket upside down and hold it over the parchment paper. The dry ice and trim fall to the bottom of the bag.

Lightly shake the dry ice and trim mix up and down, moving longitudinally along the surface of the table so the falling kief creates a trail several feet long.

As you do this the kief dust will fall down from the bag onto the paper, amid little puffs of evaporating carbon dioxide. Keep shaking for 30 seconds to sieve the trichomes through the filter. You will notice that the first glands are a pale golden-yellow and that as the process continues the trail of glands gets greener, because more vegetative material is in the mix. The first material to fall, the golden glands, is the highest quality.

Use a scraper to collect the kief, which should smell phenomenal, and store it in a clean, glass jar.

Repeat the process using the 220-micron bag, and collect the kief.

One ounce of dried sugar leaf trim yields about four grams of kief at 160 microns, and six more lower-grade grams of kief at 220 microns.

Tips

- Dry ice sieving kief sends weed dust everywhere unless the bucket bottom, where the screen is, is kept close to the table surface.

- Avoid working in areas with breezes.

- Use thinner chunks of dry ice and less agitation for purer kief.

- Use quality nylon mesh bubble bags. Plastic mesh bags degrade under the brutal cold of the dry ice.

- If you are making your own device, use stainless steel mesh rather than nylon. The nylon wears and chips when it's frozen by the dry ice. Stainless steel lasts indefinitely.

- You can use either dried or fresh-frozen trim. Both kief out nicely, and the fresh-frozen contains more terpenes.

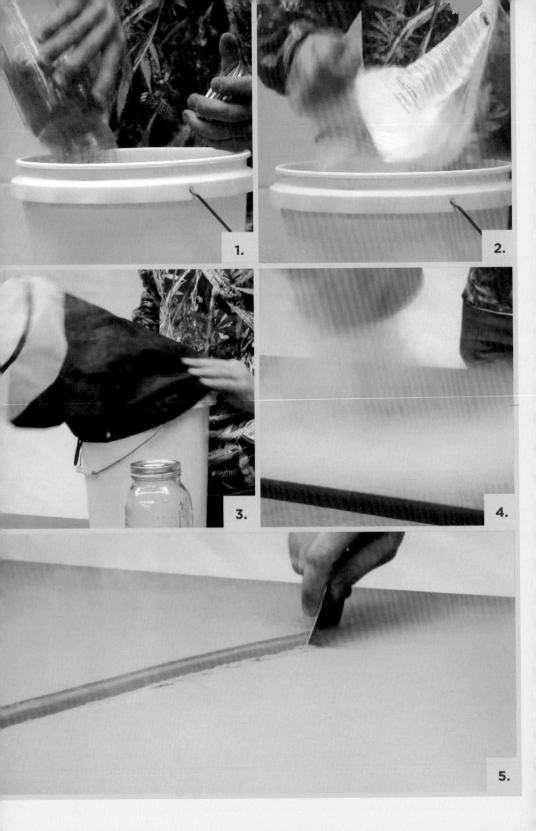

1.

2.

3.

4.

5.

6.

7.

How to Make Dry Ice Kief (Hash)

1. Place 4 oz brittle dry grass in a 5-gal bucket.

2. Add 3 lb of dry ice—it should be ice cube size or smaller. Let the mixture cool for 2 minutes.

3. Place a 220-mesh screen bag over the bucket top.

4. Turn the bucket upside down and start shaking it vigorously, moving down a 6- or 8-foot table or countertop in about 2 minutes.

5. The powder changes color from a golden to a greenish tint over the table length—golden is the purest, highest quality. The powder was separated into higher and lower quality portions.

6. The two piles—they are ready to be smoked, pressed, or used in recipes.

7. A pile of fine, blonde, dry ice hash beckons all to take a toke.

Photos: The Friday 420 Show Produced by Ryan Munevar
(See the "Dry Ice Hash Demo" video on YouTube by the Friday 420 Show.)

DRY ICE KIEF—THE MACHINE METHOD

Moving to a larger scale, Friendly Farms of California makes a portable extraction machine for dry ice sieving cannabis.

Equipment

- 2 lb of fresh or several ounces of dry trim

- Extraction Contraption cone with bracket

- Portable electric cement mixer

- 10 lb of dry ice

- Cold-resistant gloves

Method

This method is very simple. Fill the mixer with 2 lb of any mix of dry leaf/trim/ground buds and 10 lb of dry ice cubes or small pieces. Affix the Extraction Contraption cone with a bracket.

Turn on and angle the mixer so the cone faces down. The device will turn, mixing the dry ice and trim. The Extraction Contraption comes with

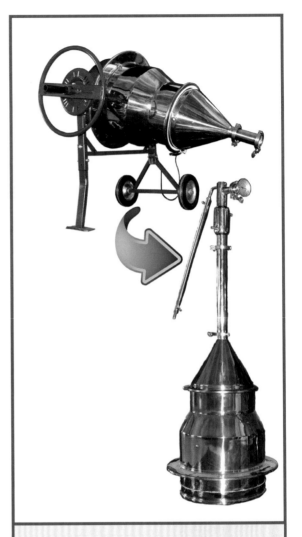

The Extraction Contraption flash freezes the trichomes on the plant, knocks them off, filters, and then collects them. Adding the Reflux Tower allows for steam distillation and the ability to distill high-grade alcohol from a variety of products giving the oil maker options on flavor/taste. This alcohol can be used to wash the heavier waxes and oils to achieve a clean extract.

Photo: Friendly Farms

screens of 75 through 150 microns to allow the glands to pass through while catching everything else.

After one minute, turn off the mixer. Remove the catcher, and open it up. The fine dry powder inside may be the finest kief you have encountered. This is the notorious One-Minute Dry Ice Kief. It contains almost no vegetation, only the pure glands. It glows pale yellow. Remove the kief just extracted.

Return the cone to the extractor several times for two- and three-minute hash. By the fourth cycle the hash is seriously green and no longer a pleasurable smoke. It can be used for further extractions and cooking. After turning for 10 minutes almost all the glands have been removed.

This method extracts THC from 3% leaf to create 30% kief. It yields between 60 to 112 grams of kief per pound of material. It has one of the easiest cleanups, since dry ice evaporates into the air and leaves nothing wet behind. A wipe down is usually all that is necessary. If convenient, extract the kief in a greenhouse or grow room during the lit period. The plants will use the evaporating CO_2.

The Extraction Contraption pairs with a still that uses grain alcohol solvent to create more refined, dabable products.

Tips

- Different strains yield kief with slightly different odors, flavors, tastes, and colors.

- This method works with dry trim, but works best with fresh sugar leaf.

- Yield and quality remain inversely related. Slight agitation and narrow filtering result in the purest kief, but yield less. Lots of agitation and a wide screen results in the most yield, but the resulting kief has more impurities and is less potent.

A PRESSING ISSUE: KIEF AND HASH

Kief can be used in a number of ways. The glands are delicious smoked fresh and loose and have a lighter, distinctively different flavor than the whole bud. Some traditionalists insist that kief is best pressed into hash. Smoking hash made with first-grade kief is an excellent experience. Many manufacturers now produce small cylindrical metal devices marketed as "pollen presses" that make clean and easy work of the process for small amounts. Just fill the press with

kief, close, and apply pressure. The harder the kief is pressed, the darker the final product. The pressure creates chemical changes in the kief as the glands rupture, which alters the taste and even the effect.

Chapter 4 explains how to make hash from kief, which is one of the cheapest and easiest ways to make hash at home. Kief can be processed into tinctures (chapter 9) or capsules (chapter 10). Kief is also great for cooking (chapter 11) because it lacks the strong green flavor that some people find unpleasant in cannabis foods and it is easier to digest.

Screening for kief, whether manually or with the help of a machine, is a fabulous way to recycle plant material that was destined for the garbage can. It is less labor intensive, less expensive, and less time consuming for the yield than most other processes.

Bowl of Hash.

Photo: Ed Rosenthal

Chapter 3.

Water Hash—
How It All Works

Water hash is a favorite method of making concentrates all over the world. Its name comes from the efficient water process that is used to collect glands from the trim, leaf, and bud bits. Water hash is actually a loose, kief-type product that can be smoked as is, or pressed into traditional hashish form. Either way, many people are quickly converted once they've experienced this pure and potent product.

Water hash can be made in small or large quantities.

Purple Emergency bubble.

Photo: Nadim Sabella Photography

Ready-made systems can be purchased to simplify the process. These systems have increased the precision and efficiency of the water hash process, and contributed to its surge in popularity. It is also possible to make water hash using home-gathered equipment.

Water hash's two-decade run of dominance is now being challenged by the rise of solvent hash. Wax, shatter, budder, and oil have muscled aside bubble hash on many dispensary shelves in the United States over the last few years. But the competition from solvent hash has also forced water hash makers to up their game. Ultra-fine water hash is now being pitched as "solventless" wax, reflecting the level of distrust about poorly made butane-tainted products. High-grade water hash is also great for edibles, and the best of it is indeed dabable. It's hard to get hurt making water hash because the method doesn't cause explosions and doesn't involve sketchy chemicals.

HOW WATER HASH WORKS

The water hash method uses a combination of water, ice, and agitation to separate glands from the plant material. Ice, water, and plant material are placed in a bucket that has been lined with bags. These filtration bags are similar to the screens used in making kief. They filter the glands by micron size, separating the trash from the hash. A micron is one-millionth of a meter, or .001 millimeters (see Glands and Screens for more info). The material is stirred to knock the trichomes free. Plant material is trapped and floats in the top bag, while the glands, which are heavy and sink, are collected in the lower bag.

Ready-made systems use multiple bags that sort the glands into grades. Unlike kief making, the material is separated in one step rather than through

Water hash 20X magnification.

Water hash 200X magnification.

Photos: Steep Hill Halent

repeated sieving. Usually the material is processed once. Some commercial hash makers process it a second time to capture more of the THC.

The ice serves a dual purpose, as an agitator against which the material is rubbed, and to make the material very cold, so the glands and the plant material remain brittle. After the material is agitated in ice water, it is allowed to settle. Then the bags are separated, and the glands are removed from each one. After the water hash is dried, it is ready to smoke. (See the "Ask Ed Grow Tip: Hash Making" video on YouTube.)

Bubble Hash (water).

Photo: Ed Rosenthal

Water hash varies in color, much like kief. The finest grade is typically a light tan, while the coarser second-tier material is slightly darker and may be a little green from plant material contamination. Many people are surprised by some fine hashes that melt and bubble when smoked.

The quality of water hash, especially from the finest grade material, is impressive. It can test as high as many solvent hash products, up to 80%. Of course, the high produced from water hash depends upon the strain and quality of the plants being used. Processing plant material with water yields hash that has been washed free of contaminants: green plant matter, mold, fungi, and chemicals.

It is possible to extract a quarter-ounce to 1 ounce of hash from every 8 ounces of plant material. The yield depends in part on the number of glands present on the material. Buds and A+ trim have a higher concentration of THC trichomes, so their yields are higher.

The entire process takes three to six hours to complete. The bag method is kind of like doing the laundry; it does not require constant attention, but it is something that you keep coming back to at regular intervals. This chapter covers the main methods for making water hash. The next chapter covers pressing it.

You can make water hash without a bag system. One method agitates the material in ice and water. The bulk of the plant material floats and is removed with a colander. The material that sinks to the bottom of the container is mostly glands. It looks grayish or tan in the water. It is rinsed out of the container and captured in a coffee filter.

WATER HASH BASICS

All gland-bearing plant material can be used to make water hash, including leaf, trim, buds, shake, or any combination of the four. The material works best when it has been dried first, although it is also possible to use fresh plant material. The Advanced Hash chapter details the use of fresh-frozen trim.

More importantly, the processes work best when the material is cold. Heat is the enemy in making bubble hash, because low temperatures are what make trichomes brittle enough to snap off, and keep the terpenes from vaping off at room temperature.

Humidity is also a basic factor. In humid areas, it is a good idea to store dried material in the freezer to avoid deterioration or molds. When using material that has not been stored in this way, place the material in the freezer until it gets cold.

Since glands reside on the surfaces of the plant, the material does not need to be ground to make water hash. Small cuttings or coarsely chopped material is most convenient. Remove any big twigs or stems, as well as twist ties, as they can tear the bags.

Whether using a ready-made bag system or materials from your kitchen, the basic principles of making water hash are the same. Aside from your technique, patience, and skill, other factors that determine the quality of the hash you produce are the caliber of the plant material and the quality of the filter.

READY-MADE BAGS

For water hash, the ready-made bag systems are a great way to go. These bags can be used over and over again. The two most popular models, the Ice-O-Lator and Bubble Bags, are both well-made systems that should give consistent results and withstand the test of time.

The Ice-O-Lator comes from Mila Jansen at the Pollinator Company, and Bubble Bags are from Fresh Headies in Canada.

Both systems provide high-quality bags that are durable, and easy to clean and use. The bags are color-coded for convenience. Bubble Bags may be more commonly known in North America because the company is based in Canada, while the Ice-O-Lator system hails from Amsterdam and is more widely known in Europe, but both products are available internationally.

The Ice-O-Lator

Mila Jansen's first invention was the Pollinator, which is discussed in chapter 4. Her interest in improving hash-making methods also led her to develop the ready-made water extraction system called the Ice-O-Lator.

The Ice-O-Lator agitates the vegetation in ice water to remove glands.

Photo: Pollinator

According to Mila, experiments with a water process did not yield much, literally, until a product called the Extractor was released in 1997. This machine was sold from the United States and manufactured in Yugoslavia. After trying it out, Mila carried the Extractor for a short time in her sales line. While this machine was a conceptual breakthrough in water hash processing, its design left something to be desired. The Extractors that were sold had mechanical difficulties and left Mila dealing with unhappy customers who had broken-down systems within a year.

The failure of the Extractor led Mila to experiment with her own design, using the principles by which the Extractor worked. She created a simpler, manual system that is called the Ice-O-Lator. This bag system first became available in 1998. It has since been refined and expanded to include three standard sizes that can process 200 to 1200 grams of material at a time, plus a travel Ice-O-Lator and a large system that can be used in the washing machine. Pollinator also makes its own washing machines in five-gallon and twenty-gallon sizes.

The Ice-O-Lator bag system consists of two bags, which line a sealable bucket of the appropriate size. Ice and water are added and then the dried material is placed in the bucket. A standard kitchen mixer affixed through the bucket's lid agitates the material. The top bag holds all of the vegetative matter. Glands filter through the silk screen of the first bag and collect in the finer screen of the second bag. The remaining water in the bucket will have particulate vegetative matter, including some nutrients that make it good for watering houseplants or vegetable gardens.

Prices for Ice-O-Lator systems range between 80 and 200 euros and they can be shipped anywhere in the world.

Bubble Bags

Bubble Bags are the design of Fresh Headies in Canada. Bubbleman, the head hash master of Fresh Headies, has traveled extensively, spreading the good word on water hash. He can also be found moderating in online forums on this topic.

Bubble Bags are available in one-gallon, five-gallon, and twenty-gallon sizes. The two larger sizes can be bought as a three-bag or eight-bag filtration system. Bubble Bags range in price from $110 U.S. for the one-gallon system to just under $500 for the twenty-gallon, eight-bag system.

There are several other brands of bags. The eight-bag system separates hash into finer categories. The size difference between just-ripe THC glands and overly mature or premature ones allows them to be separated into grades.

Bubble Bags work in a similar but slightly modified way from the Ice-O-Lator system. First, the coarse filter bag is secured in a bucket, and the water, ice, and plant material are added. The material is agitated using a kitchen mixer or a drill with a paint-mixing attachment. Purists deplore this much agitation, however. After

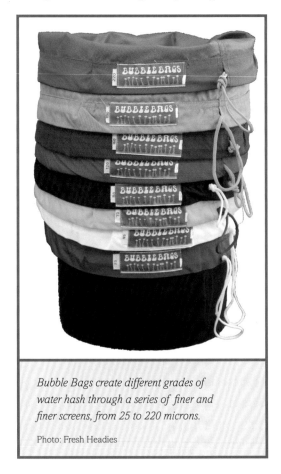

Bubble Bags create different grades of water hash through a series of finer and finer screens, from 25 to 220 microns.

Photo: Fresh Headies

the material settles, the starter bag is pulled out and squeezed. The bulk of the plant material now held in this bag is set aside. This material can be processed again. The resulting product will be lower grade, suitable for cooking.

Line the empty bucket with the additional bags. The finest bag goes in first, so it will be on the bottom. The green water is poured into the bucket, lined with the filtering bags. Pull the bags out one by one, and collect the material in the bottom of each one. Allow the kief to dry. Toss the water out or use it for watering plants.

Platinum Diesel Water Hash.

Photo: Nadim Sabella Photography

HOMEMADE BAGS

It is possible to make your own bags, or to make a smaller amount of water hash without using bags at all. To make bags, acquire silk screen in the appropriate mesh size. Standard silk-screen material is available in several size increments between the desired 100 to 150 strands per inch.

The screen must be attached to a tightly woven, water-resistant material (nylon works well) so that the silk screen forms the bottom of the bag. Multiple bags can be made with different screening levels in the 50- to 150-micron range for separating the water hash by quality.

The finest screen produces the purest hash. Multiple bags should be designed to fit inside one another, with the finest mesh bag being the largest, and the coarsest mesh bag being the smallest. A separate bag made for coarse filtering (200–250-micron-sized gaps) is also good for separating out the bulk of the vegetation in the first phase. This bag should line the bucket. It does not get layered with the other bags, so it should be as large as the bucket allows.

THE BUCKET METHOD

The essentials of the water hash method are the same, whether using a ready-made system or working from your own homemade bags.

Equipment

- Ice
- Cold water
- Hydrogen peroxide
- 2 buckets with at least one lid
- Dried trim/bud/leaf material
- Handheld mixer or drill with paint-mixing attachment
- Ready-made bag system or homemade bags
- Long rubber gloves
- Large towel
- Roll of paper towels
- Spoon or plastic card

Method

First, the buckets and equipment should be cleaned and sterilized. Mix 10 ounces (1¼ cups) of 3% hydrogen peroxide per quart of water to make a rinse.

If you are using a bag in the first round, place this bag in the bucket. Add equal amounts of ice and water until the bucket is two-thirds full. Add the prepared plant material. Wearing the long rubber gloves, use your hands to submerse it evenly in the ice water. Up to 3½ ounces (100 g) of plant material can be used in a five-gallon bucket.

If a kitchen mixer is being used, holes are punched in a bucket lid to accommodate the mixing attachments. This keeps the material from sloshing out while it is being agitated. It also allows the mixer to run hands-free.

Using the tool of choice (kitchen mixer or drill with paint-mixing attachment), agitate the material for 15 minutes, and then allow the mixture to settle. If using a ready-made system, the speed recommended in the instructions should be used. As a general rule of thumb, lower speeds work well when mixing amounts under five gallons. Medium to high speeds are better when using a system that is five gallons or larger. As it is mixed, the material becomes frothy. You may want to remove the suds before recommencing.

Blend the material up to four times for 15 minutes at a time. Mixing the material more times produces higher yields, but also results in more particulate vegetative matter. Longer times produce less pure results, especially if multiple bags aren't separating the hash into grades. When using a single collection mechanism, a shorter time should be used on the first round. After this hash is collected, the plant material can be reprocessed using a longer mixing time. Multiple bags allow the material to be processed all at once without sacrificing a high-grade collection.

Once the last mixing round is completed, let the mixture sit for at least 30 minutes. This allows the glands time to sink into the collection filters. If all of the ice has melted, more can be added. In cold weather, the bucket can be set outside to keep the mixture cold.

Once the material has settled, it is time to separate out the glands. If the agitation has been done inside a bag, pull out this bag, removing the bulk of the plant material. The bucket now contains green water with silt in the bottom. This silt is the water hash and a small amount of particulate vegetative matter.

Line the second bucket with the collection bag or bags. The finest mesh bag goes on the bottom, so it is added to the bucket first. The coarsest bag is the last bag added, so it is the top layer. The first bag has separated out everything over the 200–250-micron size, depending on its mesh size. Now the successive layers of the bags will do the grading for you.

Pour the water into the bucket that is lined with the filter bags. Slowly lift out each bag, allowing time for the water to drain. Be patient. If the entire bottom of the bag seems to be clogged, it may be necessary to reach in and gently push some material to the side. Stir up the material as little as possible.

After each bag is removed, lay it on the towel and pat off excess water. More water can be removed by wrapping it with towels and squeezing it. The inside of each bag contains some tan to brown silt-like material. Carefully arrange

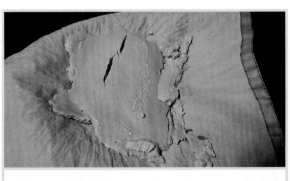

Wet water hash drying.

Photo: A-Bear Concentrates

the bag so that the material is accessible. Blot the material off with a paper towel. Remove it from the bag using a credit card or a spoon. If multiple bags were used, keep the grades separated.

Place the material in a flat-bottomed bowl, or on a plate or other surface where it can be

1. 2.

3. 4.

5. 6.

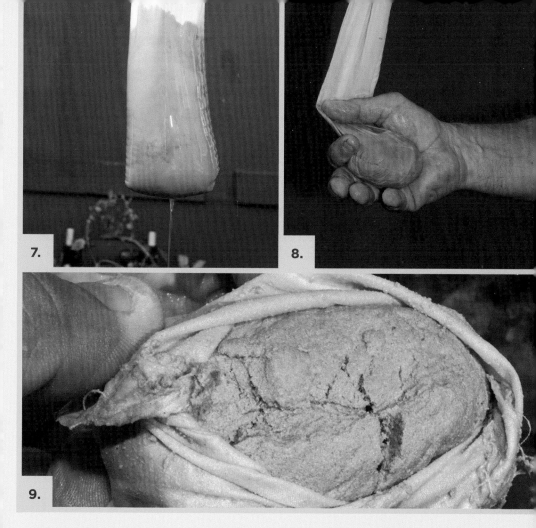

7.

8.

9.

How to Make Water Hash (Bubble)

1. 5 lb of frozen grass is cut using a very sharp knife.

2. The grass is placed in a 30-gal bucket.

3. The bucket is filled to about 2 inches above the grass with cold water. Then add 15 lb of ice.

4. The grass/water/ice combo is thoroughly agitated using a drill with a paint mixer attachment. Wait 15 minutes. Using a colander, scoop up all of the vegetative material that is floating on top (not shown).

5. This specially sewn silk screen bag is placed over another container.

6. Using a convenient container (such as a cooking pot or a pail) pour the remaining water through a screen into the second bucket.

7. The water and vegetative particles flow through, leaving the glands in the silk screen sleeve.

8. The glands form a ball at the bottom of the sleeve.

9. The glands are gathered from the sleeve and squeezed dry using a cloth. The hash needs to dry, but is usable immediately.

Photos: Ed Rosenthal
(See the "Ask Ed Grow Tip: Hash Making" video on YouTube.)

left to dry, then put it in a cool, dark place where it will get some airflow, but won't blow away once dry. The material will dry in about 12 hours, but allow a full week to dry and cure fully. Even if some material is used sooner, allow the moisture to evaporate from the remaining material so it is not susceptible to mold.

THE COFFEE FILTER METHOD

This method works well for small-scale water hash production and uses common kitchen equipment. Chop the plant material to a coarsely ground consistency. Cone-type coffee makers look like a pointier version of a standard coffeemaker basket. They are inexpensive and are available at kitchenware stores, some gourmet coffee shops, grocery stores, or on the web. The #4 size or larger is recommended. Both reusable and disposable filters for these cones are available at the same shops where the cone was purchased.

This method yields nice hash, but the process is not controlled by precise micron-sized filters. There is also no final filtration of small vegetative matter, so the product is not as pure as the hash made in a bag system. Still, the water hash produced using this method equals the quality of dry-screened kief.

WATER HASH TIPS

- Fresh-frozen material works best. If the material was not stored in the freezer, place it in the freezer until it is cold. If you have too much material to place it in the freezer, use extra ice. Place a few inches of water in the bucket, add the plant material, and fill the remainder of the bucket with ice. Allow the mixture to sit and cool for 30 minutes before beginning.

- It is better to use a standard two-beater mixer or drill with a paint-mixing attachment rather than a handheld or one-piece mixer because the latter do not have as much agitating power and they work by pulling material up to the spinning blade. Stringy pieces of plant material easily clog the blade.

- Don't get impatient in the final steps! Dry the material thoroughly at the end of the process. Water hash stored before it is dried molds, ruining it.

- Water and mash left over at the end of the process contain nutrients present in the plant material. It's great for watering plants or using as a mulch or in compost.

Equipment

- Ice
- Cold water
- Dried plant material (coarsely ground)
- Blender
- Mixing bowl
- Colander or wire mesh strainer
- Cone-type single cup coffee maker
- Reusable metal cone coffee filter, or silk screen
- Coffee filters
- 2–3 large glass jars with tight-sealing lids
- Dish towel
- Paper towels
- Scraping tool (spoon, credit card, or business card)

Method

Place enough plant material in the blender to fill it halfway. Add ice and cold water in equal amounts until the blender is full. Turn the blender on at full speed for 45 seconds to 1 minute. Let the mixture settle. Repeat three or four times. The more times the blender is run, the higher the yield; however, more vegetative material will also become particulate and lower the purity of the results.

Pour the mixture from the blender through a colander or strainer into a mixing bowl. Bowls designed to pour, such as a pancake batter bowl or an 8-cup measuring cup, work best. This step separates out the bulk of the plant material.

Now pour this water through the reusable coffee filter into the glass jars, until they are about two-thirds full. Quart-sized, sealable, glass canning jars work well. Material will collect in the coffee filter. This is the smaller vegetative matter. The glands are too small to stay in the reusable coffee filter and have passed with the water into the glass jars. Pour another cup or two of water through the filter into the glass jars to wash out any remaining glands.

Seal the jars and place them in the refrigerator for an hour. The glands settle and form silt at the bottom of the jar. Tapping the jar lightly a few times on a tabletop helps settle some of the floating material.

Gently remove the jars from the refrigerator without stirring up the material that has collected at the bottom and pour off the top one-half to two-thirds of the water. The goal is to retain the glands that are gathered in the bottom, while removing as much water content as possible.

Set up the cone on top of a suitable container such as a quart jar. Drain the remaining water and silt through the coffee filter with a disposable filter paper. The flow of water through the filter slows as the material collects, but allow it to drain completely.

Carefully remove the paper coffee filter from the cone. Flatten it with the material inside by patting it with a towel.

Material can be dried either before or after it is collected from the coffee filter. Drying it inside the coffee filter takes a little longer, but the hash is protected from blowing away and is easier to remove from the paper when both are dry. To dry in the coffee filter, place it atop a layer of paper or cloth towels. Once it is dry split the filter along a seam.

Collect the material using a spoon or plastic or paper card. Allow the material to fully dry before pressing or storing, which takes a day or two depending on the environmental conditions and the amount being dried.

To make more than one batch at a time combine the blender water in a large container and let the water settle, or use several bowls, let the kief settle in each one, then combine them.

Some Tips

Use a siphon rather than a pour to remove one-half to two-thirds of the water from the container. This gives you more control and creates less turbulence, so the silt at the container bottom is not disturbed. Use clean, flexible aquarium tubing. Place the other end of the tubing into a sink or other drainage area.

Heat speeds up the drying process. Use a propagation mat used to sprout seedlings—it will maintain a 74°F (23°C) temperature—or a heating pad set on low. Place the mat under a towel and put the drying water hash on top. Food dehydrators set on low are another effective controlled heat source.

THE JAR SHAKER METHOD

The simplest method for making water hash is using a homemade shaker. This method is the easiest in terms of time and equipment, but it also produces the least amount of hash, and the product won't be as pure as with methods using micron-gauged filtering bags. Manual agitation is more labor intensive, but it requires no electricity and can be accomplished anywhere that the materials can be gathered.

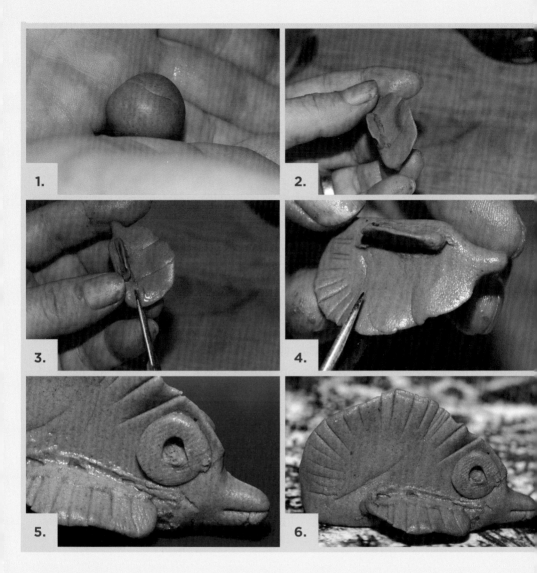

Making Hashimals

1. In the beginning, there was a ball of water hash.

2. It was rolled into a cylinder, flattened, and then shaped.

3. Further shaping using an awl.

4. Creating the top fin.

5. Close-up of the hashimal.

6. The hashimal is complete. Fortunately, it was destroyed in intentional fires.

Photos: Ed Rosenthal

Equipment

- Up to an ounce of brittle, dry trim, bud bits, or shake
- Water
- Ice
- Sealable glass jar
- Colander or wire mesh strainer
- Slotted spoon or tea strainer
- Coffee cone (#4)
- Paper coffee filters
- Dish towel
- Paper towels
- Scraping tool (spoon, credit card, or business card)

Method

Reduce the marijuana material to a coarse powder, similar to dried cooking herbs like oregano or basil, using a marijuana or coffee grinder or blender for a very short time.

Place the material in the jar, up to one-quarter full. Pint, quart, and two-quart jars all work. Add equal amounts of ice and very cold water until the jar is almost full. Leave about an inch of space at the top of the jar, then seal it and shake for 10 minutes.

Pour the water/material mix into a bowl and put it in the refrigerator to allow it to settle for an hour. Most of the ice may melt in this time.

Remove the floating plant material with a tea strainer or slotted spoon. The plant material can be saved and reprocessed. Manual shaking does not remove all trichomes on the first round.

Once the plant material has been removed, allow the silt to resettle at the bottom of the bowl for 15–20 minutes. Drain off one-half to two-thirds of the water slowly, with an eye to saving all of the silt-like water hash material in the bottom of the jar.

Set up the cone lined with a paper coffee filter. Pour the remaining contents of the bowl through the cone. As the water hash collects in the bottom of the filter, the water will drain more slowly. Allow all of the water to drain from the filter. Then remove the filter from the cone, allowing it to flatten with the wet hash inside. Set it on a dish towel and carefully remove as much water as possible by pressing with the towel or paper towels.

Split the coffee filter along the seam and open it like a butterfly spreads its wings. Collect the material inside using a spoon or card to scrape it loose from the paper. The material is easier to separate from the coffee filter when it

The material can dry either before or after it is removed from the filter. Even if some of the material is collected for use before the drying completes, the water hash should be allowed to air dry over a day or two to reduce the chance of mold. After the water hash is dry, it can be used, stored, or pressed into hash.

PRESSING AND STORAGE

Some people find the aroma and flavor of water hash unusually mild. Water filters out some of the water-soluble chlorophyll and other pigments, as well as some of the terpenes, which give marijuana its taste and

Bubba Kush water hash.

Photo: Nadim Sabella Photography

scent. The milder qualities of water hash are not an indication of its potency. If a stronger aroma or flavor is desired, Bubbleman recommends pressing some dry-sifted kief with the bubble hash.

When smoked fresh, high-purity water hash bubbles and melts, hence the description, "full melt" bubble hash. Because of how it reacts when burned, water hash may need to be pressed lightly in order to smoke through a standard pipe. People often press the material in their hands to form balls or triangles. A more thorough press to form a true hashish piece is explained in the next chapter.

Water hash stores best in loose form. Keep it in a sealed container away from light and heat until ready for use.

Bubba Kush bubble hash.

Photo: Bubbleman

Chapter 4.

Advanced Hash—

Beyond the Basics

Concentrated cannabis may be the future of marijuana as a medicine and as a recreational substance. You've read about how water and ice can be used to mechanically separate trichomes from the plant, and filters can concentrate the glands into unpressed hash. Now you'll see these processes are further refined using machinery and tighter control of temperature and humidity to yield the strongest nonsolvent

Nonsolvent extracts.

Photo: Pollinator

concentrates. We'll also detail pressing classic hashish, which is a collection of marijuana's resinous glands compressed into balls, cakes, or slabs.

The origins of hashish date back millennia and are believed to have begun in Asia, near the Hindu Kush region. Hash making has a long tradition in many countries near the 30th latitude, including India, Nepal, Afghanistan, Pakistan, and Lebanon.

Making hashish is a two-step process. In step one, the glands are collected. All collection methods yield a consumable product, but it is not yet hashish. Hashish involves a second step: compressing the collected material into bricks or balls.

Sifting for kief is the primary low-tech way to collect glands for hash. Water hash can be pressed using the same methods. Another method of collection—hand rubbing—dates back to ancient times. While low in yield, this often produces extremely high-quality hash. Hand-rubbed hash is collected fresh from the plant, and the resin is still sticky, so the method of pressing involves a slightly different process.

Several kinds of hash, including Nepalese Temple Balls, Blonde Lebanese, and Afghani slabs.

Photo: Ed Rosenthal

Pressing hash involves a combination of force and mild heat to condense the glands into a solid mass. The shape and size of hash varies depending on the pressing method. When hand pressed, hash is often ball-shaped. Flat-pressed hash may look like thin shale rock, with hardened shelf-like layers that chip along the creases. Mechanically pressed hash is usually a neat cake, like a bar of soap. Hashish ranges in color and pliability. The variety of marijuana used, manufacturing method, temperature, and the purity of the kief influence

Mechanically pressed hash.

Photo: DoobieDuck.com

its color, which ranges from light yellow-tan to charcoal black, and its texture, which ranges from pliable taffy to hard and brittle.

Hashish oxidizes and darkens from exposure to light, oxygen, and heat. Regardless of its texture, high-quality hash should soften with the simple warmth of your hands.

Aficionados often describe the high that hash produces as more complex than that of kief. In the region of traditional hash making, kief is typically aged, sometimes for a year or more, before it is pressed. Most modern hash makers do not wait that long.

Full melt bubble hash.

Photo: Steep Hill Halent

WHAT IS HASHISH?

Ask Ed

Ed:
What exactly is hash?

Shales
Oakland, California

Shales:

Hashish, or hash, is a conglomeration of crushed and heated glands or trichomes. Using gentle heat and pressure the gland heads' membranes break, releasing the viscous liquid. The pressure forces out the air, leaving the pure mass of crushed glands.

Hash can be made as easily as placing some kief in cellophane, wrapping it carefully, and then placing it inside the heel of your shoe. Walk and stand on it for 15–30 minutes, and unwrap the newly pressed hash. A friend showed me how he makes it using a thin cotton cloth to wrap the kief. Then he presses it using a dry iron. Commercially, hash is made using high-power presses. The most sophisticated of these units heats the material in addition to applying pressure.

TIP: Unpressed kief oxidizes in warm temperatures, while hash is more resilient to warmth, so long as it is pressed when it is totally dry. When pressed wet, however, hash molds. You can store material in its unpressed form in a cool, dark place. Once pressed, hash stored in the freezer suffers little from aging.

INTRODUCTION TO ADVANCED WATER HASH

Water hash can be as strong as and tastier than the newer solvent hashes. In the 2013 Emerald Cup—a longtime, outdoor organic medical marijuana competition in Northern California—the first- and second-place water hash winners tested at 67% and 70% THC, a metric once thought impossible for old-school bubble hash.

Advanced water hash uses the same principles outlined in the Water Hash chapter, it just takes into account more variables, from the strain type and trichome shape to harvest methods and ambient temperature and humidity in the washing room.

Converted cold-water washing machine being loaded with trim to make hash.

THE MACHINE METHOD

There are several key principles for producing the highest-quality, dabable water hash.

First, trichomes must be treated gently. Mechanical agitation in the ice-bath stage is needed, but it's also the enemy. Paint mixers are too rough for award-winning bubble. Use a special machine such as the Bubbleator (from the Pollinator Company), the Bubble Now, or the gentle cycle on a washing machine modified by removing its filters.

Second, heat is an enemy. It can dry out buds and sap them of their flavors and strength. During drying, high temperatures vaporize the hash's great flavors. Storing hash at a high temperature degrades its flavor and potency.

The result of paying attention to the fundamentals of the process is phenomenal. High-grade water hash is being rebranded as "solventless wax." It gives consumers who want to dab a tasty, effective option that doesn't involve explosive solvents.

Equipment

- 20-gallon Bubble Now, Bubble Magic Extraction Machine, Bubbleator, or top-loading washing machine

- Bubble Bags (microns—220 zippered to hold the grass in the washer; 160, the first filter, removes contaminants; 73 for low-grade; 25 for high-grade)

- Cannabis (1000 to 2500 grams, frozen, high-trichome leaf)

- Water (filtered for best results)

- Ice—enough to fill the machine 60% full, and refill it as it melts

- 20-gallon bucket

- Alcohol or hydrogen peroxide

- Gloves

- Spoon

- Sieve

- Parchment paper

- Thick cardboard

Bubbleator.

Photo: Pollinator

Method

Consider the best location for setting up the machine. The best situation is a sterile lab setting. Hash is very sticky, and captures contaminants floating in the air, such as dander, dog hair, and dust. A room with filtered air is best. Outdoors, dry dusty days are a poor choice, but days after a rain when the air is clean are acceptable. The ambient temperature is best below 65°F (18°C) with low humidity—between 15% and 50%. Hash is oxidized and darkens when it is manufactured or stored for long periods at high temperatures such as 80°F to 90°F (27°C to 32°C).

Next, consider the source material. Dried, cured, sugar leaf works fine, but the best water hash is made from fresh-frozen material. Trichome-rich leaves are cut from ripe plants, bagged in Ziploc freezer bags, and frozen. Freezing locks in all the terpenes and cannabinoids present on the plant at the time of harvest, rather than losing significant amounts of both to drying, curing, and processing.

Thoroughly disinfect the machine, hose, bags, and buckets using hydrogen peroxide.

Line your 20-gallon bucket with filter bags, starting with the finest 25-micron bag and ending with the biggest 160-micron bag.

Place the machine's outflow hose into the filter bucket.

Place a base layer of ice in the machine.

Fit the open, 220-micron bag in the machine and add the material.

Fill the bag half-full with nine parts trim to one part ice. Alternate adding trim and ice. Zip up and tie the top of the bag, and pour more ice over the bag until the ice level reaches eight inches below the rim of the machine.

Next, add water until it's four inches below the surface of the ice. Wait 15 minutes for the trim to soak up the water, then add more ice and water, until the water is below the ice's surface level, and the ice is eight inches below the rim of the metal basin. Leave room for the mixture to agitate.

Turn the machine on gentle and monitor the agitation. Use wooden spoons to help the bag settle into the ice bath. Add more ice and water as the ice melts and settles. The color of the water should turn completely gold quickly. On a standard washing machine, use the gentle cycle. DO NOT let the device automatically drain. Run two gentle agitation cycles—*then* let it drain.

During this ice-cold agitation process, the brittle, frozen trichomes will have snapped off the leaf, traveled through the lining of the 220-micron "garbage" bag, and into the ice bath. The water turns green and the plant oils make the surface of the water frothy.

After agitation, the machine pumps the trichome-rich water out of the washer basin and into the filter bags, which are set up inside the 20-gallon bucket.

The inside of the bucket will be foamy with cannabis oils. Jiggle the bucket gently to help water pass through the filters and use filtered ice water in a small pump sprayer to rinse the trichomes off the bag's sides and down and through the 160-micron filter.

Start pulling the bags up one at a time.

First pull out the "garbage" bag. The material inside the bottom of the bag looks like green silt. Rinse down the edges, get everything collected in the bottom, and pull out the garbage.

Pull the second bag, then spray, jiggle, and repeat. The 73–160-micron stuff is a little green, but not as green as the first bag. Keep pulling, spraying, and jiggling until it's all collected in the middle of the mesh. Trichomes smaller than 70 microns pass through the mesh but everything from 73 to 160 microns will be collected. (The sweet spot for trichomes is 70 to 160 microns, with tinier ones better for dabbing, and the bigger stuff more suitable for edibles.)

73-micron hash.

90-micron hash.

Photos: David Downs

Pull up the bag to the top and spoon out the green-colored wet paste onto parchment paper set on a towel or thick cardboard, or something else that will safely wick moisture away.

The next bag catches the vast bulk of trichomes between 25 and 73 microns. The material in here is both green contaminant and gold trichomes. The goal is to push the green through the screen while holding on to the gold.

Pull the bag up; it'll be heavy with water, its pores clogged with trichomes. Much like panning for gold, you want to lightly spin the emulsion while spraying down the sides. The mesh holds on to the glands while the fine green particles fall through with the water. Keep spraying, rotating, and pulling until the green is gone and it just looks like a bunch of golden sand.

Remove this light clay-like wet hash from the mesh and place it on a drying surface. Once the bottom of the mesh bag is scraped clean of any remaining hash, use a sieve and spoon to redistribute and aerate the drying hash on a wider surface area.

You will have two piles: the 25–73-micron pile, which is full melt suitable for smoking, and the 73–160-micron pile, which is great for baking.

Leave it to cure for 12 to 24 hours. It's done when it is totally dry and crumbly between your gloved hands.

Drying

There's a compromise in drying—trying to remove moisture from the hash without also vaporizing off the delicious yet volatile essential oils, or terpenes. Use a spoon to break up the wet clumps of hash and spread it evenly on parchment paper on a thick cardboard drying board.

Drying should be done in a room with a temperature between 40°F (4°C) and 68°F (20°C). The reason for the low temperature is that some terpenes evaporate at 70°F (21°C).

Humidity is also a factor, with sub-30% humidity being optimal, but it can vary by strain.

Under magnification, the final product will look like sandy heaps of full, sticky, oily, trichome heads. Store in a cool, dark place, and don't press until the material is completely dry.

Tips

- Check the seams to make sure your bubble bags are not inside out.

- Inspect the machine output hose line for leaks.

- Use a gravity-based system with suspended bags and buckets to save your back.

- Buy bags with lots of mesh area, durable sidewalls, and consistent micron spacing—cheap eBay bags often have inconsistent micron widths in the center of the mesh versus the edge.

- Keeps hands off the trichomes.

- Trim wet and freeze.

- If you make water hash often, invest in an ice-making machine.

- You don't have to use as much ice when using large cubes. They don't melt as fast as small pieces.

- Strains: Different strains yield differently sized and shaped trichomes, and differing amounts of oils and terpenes. Hashing Blue Dream versus hashing Bubba Kush is like night and day at the micron level. Blue Dream trichomes are long and thin, and you can raise the temperature and humidity during drying. Bubba Kush, Sour Diesel, and OG Kush glands are short, stocky, and oily, and need to be processed at as cold a temperature as possible and dried at 40°F (4°C) under minimal humidity to capture the resin's odors.

- Cultivation Environment: Outdoor-grown cannabis tends to have smaller trichomes (120 microns) than indoor (160).

- Bag Size and Number: This can vary. You can use as little as two 25- and 160-micron bags, plus a 220-micron garbage bag for simplicity's sake, or pull and spoon progressively narrower bands of glands and materials at 90, 73, and even 35 microns.

- Agitation: Purists sometimes use something as basic as a pole or paddle to gently hand-agitate the main bag in the bucket; the trade-off is in the yield. A 30-minute machine wash of 1,000 high-quality grams can yield as much as 112 grams of top-shelf hash. Less agitation equals purer hash but lower yield.

HASH FACTS

- The color and consistency of hash varies considerably. However, it softens and crumbles from very mild heat, even the simple body warmth created by holding it in your hands.

- The quality and potency of hash is dependent on several factors including the quality of the plant material from which it was made and the presence of moisture.

- Moisture enables molds to attack hash. It is indicated by a musty smell and by visible white streaks within the hash. Moldy hash should never be smoked or ingested. It can make you sick.

- Hash burns slowly with an incense-like fragrance. The flavor of the smoke is often peppery or slightly spicy, often with floral undertones. When burned, it produces thick, white smoke that sometimes carries a bluish tint. The resulting ash is white.

PREPARING KIEF OR WATER HASH FOR HASH MAKING

Kief and water hash methods of collection are covered thoroughly in chapters 2 and 3. While these two processes have different advantages, each yields dry, loose material that can be pressed to make hash. Before attempting to press kief or water hash, the material must be completely dry. To ensure that all moisture has been eliminated before pressing, dry the material one last time. Place the kief or water hash in a food dehydrator set on the lowest setting, a horticultural heat mat (preset at 74°F [23°C]), microwave the material on low, or place it in an open dish in a frost-free freezer. The vacuum conditions promote water evaporation, preventing mold from infecting and spoiling the hash. However, when the drying temperature is above 75°F (24°C) some of the terpenes will evaporate, costing the hash a panoply of unique odors and their effects.

Collecting hash resin.

Rubbing hand hash to create a ball.

Photos: Ed Rosenthal

COLLECTING BY HAND: RUBBING FOR HASH

There are many tales about collecting hash from fresh plants. Hand rubbing for hash has been a common gathering method for centuries in some parts of Asia, and it is still a primary way of collecting for hash in other parts of the world.

Because it requires no equipment, hand rubbing is a novel and spontaneous way to collect for hash, but this method also has several downsides.

First, the effort required to produce substantial yield is greater than with other methods. It can be messy and labor intensive. Second, hash collected this way contains debris from plants and hands, and contains more water, making it more likely to spoil. Hand rubbing requires access

THE HAND-RUBBING TECHNIQUE

Before starting collection, coat your hands with a little cooking oil, then pat it off with a towel. The thin oil layer makes the palms a little sticky, helping to attract the first glands. It also makes removing the resin from the hands easier.

First, choose the right time of day. Early morning is not a good time if the plants are moist with dew. Wait until the day warms a bit and the plants have been under the sun long enough to be totally water-free.

Rub the plants very lightly, starting at the top of the plant and working down rubbing the topside of the leaves. Remember that the glands' heads are tiny globes supported by stalks sticking up from buds and the upper side of the leaves. Think of brushing the fine hairs of a person's arm while only barely touching the skin. Use the same technique for resin rubbing.

As soon as you start rubbing, your hands will begin to collect the sticky, tar-like resin, and the air will be filled with the plant's heady aroma. High-quality resin creates a clear sticky gloss on the palms, darkening to amber as the resin builds up. Only resin should be collecting on the hands. This is a clear indicator that you have chosen the right time to collect. Lots of pieces of plant material on the hands indicate that the plant contains dead leaves. If it isn't inconvenient, removing them before rubbing will improve the quality of the rub.

If you are collecting green material you are probably rubbing too vigorously. It is nearly impossible to avoid attracting some errant leaf bits and particles onto your sticky hands. It is tedious to remove even larger plant debris, so try to avoid collecting it with the resin.

to mature plants rather than dried trim and leaf. Unlike the other methods, it is only capable of being made at certain times in the growing cycle and cannot be made from material that has been collected and stored. Removing the collected resin from the hands can be an involved task.

Having pointed out these shortcomings, hand rubbing can be used when the goal is a small amount of quality hash to be used shortly after it is collected. Especially when the leaves and trim aren't going to be saved, hand rubbing is a good way to salvage some of the THC before or during harvest and manicuring.

The amount of material collected through hand rubbing is dependent on timing and good technique but is likely to be less than an ounce per hour. It is best to collect for hash when the plants' stigmas have just started to turn amber as they reach full maturity, but before the leafy material has become brown or dry. The more dead or dry material, such as dead leaves on the plant, the more plant debris will be mixed in with the hash. If the plants are mature and have some dead or dried material, removing these leaves before collec-

Sticky resin built up on hands is rolled into a ball of finger hash.

Photo: Ed Rosenthal

tion increases the quality of the hash. Collection should not be done when the plants are wet from watering, as this increases the water content.

Removing the Resin

Scrape the collected material from your hands periodically. Another person can help, or you can do it yourself. Use a blunt-edged scraper such as a dull dining knife. If more resin is to be collected, leave a little on the hands. Another way to remove collected resin is to rub the hands back and forth against each other, as if trying to warm them up. The resin forms into a roll.

After the material is scraped or rubbed off of the hands it is kneaded and rolled between the hands until it forms a ball. It can be worked by rolling it between your two palms. Work it for several minutes to warm it and squeeze out residual moisture.

Hand-rolled hash can be pressed further using methods described on the following pages, or it can be considered complete after it has been worked into a ball. It is better to use this hash soon after it is made rather than storing it. Because it contains fresh resins, high vegetative content, and water from the live plant, hand-rubbed hash is more vulnerable to spoilage. If stored, the best place for it is in an opaque container that is not made of plastic or rubber, placed in the freezer. Parchment paper and silicone are excellent containers.

Using water to remove resin from the hands is counterproductive, since the goal is to remove as much water as possible. Instead of aiding in the removal of the resin, water promotes spoilage.

If hash shows signs of molding, such as an acrid or mossy smell, or grainy white lines appear within the hash, it is ruined and should not be used. These bacteria and molds are no good for you.

PRESSING AND STORING HASHISH

Pressing transforms the material both chemically and physically. The glands are warmed and most break, releasing the sticky oils that contain the psychoactive cannabinoids, as well as the terpenes—the source of marijuana's smell, taste, and personality.

Terpenes lend fragrance to the hash. Smells and flavors characteristic to hashish range from spicy or peppery to floral. Many terpenes are volatile at room temperature. When inhaled they contribute to the lung expansiveness (i.e., cough factor), as well as the taste. Aged kief is both milder in smell and flavor, and less cough inducing, because some of the terpenes, not the THC, have dissipated.

Releasing and warming cannabinoids exposes them to air. This has the beneficial effect of potentiating the THC through decarboxylation. Continued exposure to light, air, heat, and moisture leads to THC deterioration.

You can press hash manually or mechanically. Manual methods work well for smaller amounts. Mechanical methods use a press, which is fast, convenient, and efficient. This section describes the best manual methods and discusses mechanical pressing.

DECARBOXYLATION EXPLAINED

In the growing plant THC is present in the form of THCA, also called THC acid. A carbonate molecule (COOH) is attached to it, which is also called a carboxyl group or acid. THC is only marginally psychoactive when a carboxyl group is attached.

Decarboxylation removes the carbonate molecule COOH by breaking its bond with the THC molecule. This occurs when material is subject to mild heat.

When the carbonate molecule bond with THC is broken, the COOH evaporates away as water vapor (H_2O) and carbon dioxide (CO_2), leaving the THC behind. This is sometimes called "potentiating" the THC because it becomes psychoactive.

Shoe Hash

This pressing method lets you multitask. While you are busy doing other things, the hash is being inconspicuously pressed within your shoe!

Shoe hash is a low-hassle way to press a small amount of kief or water hash. A few grams, usually 5 grams or less, are bagged in tightly wrapped cellophane or parchment paper wrapped around the material several times. A piece of tape stops it from unfolding. Punch a pinhole through the package to allow trapped air to escape. Don't use a plastic bag because the hash sticks to it messily. It is important for scientific as well as psychological reasons for the material to be securely sealed before it goes in your shoe.

The package is ready to place. Place it inside the heel of your shoe. Hard-soled shoes or boots are better for pressing than soft-soled shoes, such as sports shoes, which take longer to process the kief.

The heel's weight and pressure within the shoe, aided by body heat, presses the hash into a slab. The pressing takes 15 minutes to an hour of on-foot activity, but it benefits from additional wear.

Pressing by Hand

Pressing by hand is a method for transforming kief into hashish a few grams at a time. Fresh hand-rubbed resin is often pressed by hand, too.

While pressing by hand is convenient, since it requires no additional equipment, it takes considerable energy and the results are better with a practiced technique. Those unaccustomed to hand pressing may find it difficult to make the material cohere. The considerable work it takes to get well-pressed hash can easily result in sore hands.

This method works best using freshly sieved medium- to high-quality kief. If the kief contains a significant amount of vegetative material, it is harder to mold into hash and may not stick together properly.

To hand press, measure out a small mound of fresh kief that will fit comfortably in the hand. A few grams are usually the most. Work this material with one hand against the other until it begins to cohere into a solid piece. Then rub it between the palms, or between palm and thumb.

After 10 minutes or more of working the material it begins to change density. Dry, aged kief lacks some of its original stickiness and may take longer to stick together, but if it was stored properly it should coop-

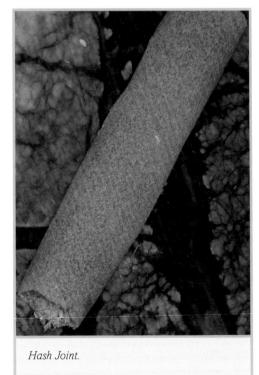

Hash Joint.

Photo: Ed Rosenthal

erate, though it may require more kneading. When a piece of hashish has not been pressed properly, it crumbles easily at room temperature.

If the kief is particularly stubborn and won't stick together to form a mass, mildly heat it. Wrap the material in food-grade cellophane, ensuring that it is completely sealed and all the air is squeezed out. Wrap this package in several layers of thoroughly wetted newspaper or cloth or paper towels. Turning frequently, warm in a skillet that is set on the lowest heat. It doesn't need to be heated as long as with other methods because the only point of heating it is to get the material to stick together so it can be kneaded into a solid piece.

Another method is to wrap it the same way and press it for a few seconds on each side with an iron that is set on a very low heat setting.

Machine Presses

Making hash is a cinch with a mechanical press. Bookbinding presses, called nipping presses, can be used. Plans are available on the web for building a press using a hydraulic jack.

Hand-pumped hydraulic presses are a less expensive way to get a tight press. Another cost-effective method uses a vice grip, although it takes some adaptation. For small amounts, a pollen press can be used in conjunction with a handheld kief-collecting grinder. Kief is added to this small metal tube. The tension pin is placed in, and the pollen press is screwed shut. The next day, the kief has been pressed into a neat hash block. Many companies have similar presses now, including one made of stainless steel with a low-torque T-handle.

This heavy-duty unit presses large amounts of kief.

Photo: TrimPro

Storage

Once the hashish is pressed, it can be kept for months or possibly years, with little deterioration to its potency and flavor, with proper storage. A frost-free freezer is the best place for storing hash.

Metal, glass, or silicone containers are preferred for storage. Plastics and rubber are not recommended because the terpenes—responsible for the flavor and aroma of the hash—are somewhat volatile compounds that interact chemically with plastic or rubber, degrading both the hash and the container. However, this happens slowly under freezing conditions.

Nothing sticks to NoGoo silicone containers. They are a must for storing and transporting concentrates.

Photo: NoGoo

Over time, the outer layer of hashish oxidizes and loses potency. The inside, not exposed to higher levels of light and oxygen, remains potent. Studies suggest that dark-colored hash degrades more rapidly than lighter-colored hash. Remember that mild light, heat, moisture, and oxygen oxidizes the outside of the hash, destroying its potency.

Chapter 5.

Vaporizers—

Handheld, Desktop, Portable, Vape Pens

Smoking is one of the most controversial aspects of cannabis use. Studies have found harmful compounds produced when bud is burned but those findings are not confirmed in population studies. The ambiguous research aside, many people would prefer not to inhale smoke from burning vegetation. While marijuana can have positive effects many people are concerned about smoking it.

Using marijuana medically raises new concerns about this contradiction. The active ingredients in marijuana, THC and the other cannabinoids, don't pose health hazards, but the tars and other compounds may, so people have sought out alternate modes of ingestion. Cooking and tinctures are obvious answers, but their delivery, onset, and effects are different than smoked marijuana.

Vaporization is the solution for some users. Vaporizing is a fantastic innovation based on the principle of evaporation. The temperature at which THC and other cannabinoids evaporate is lower than the temperature at which plant material burns. Vaporizers heat marijuana to the point where the volatile THC and terpenes evaporate, but below the temperature at which plant material burns.

Vaporizers (also known as vapes) are considered a key component of reducing harm from marijuana use. Vaporizers pass medical muster, and even appear in some hospitals. Vapes used in research pass peer reviews and are used in and tested in published studies.

Vaporizers reduce health risks associated with smoking. It may also be a more efficient use of cannabis. When marijuana is burned, up to 30% of the THC content is lost to the combustion process. Since vaporizers evaporate THC without combusting the plant material, it is possible to get more THC than with a burn.

In a leading study on the increased safety of vaporization over smoking, researchers found 111 different molecules in smoked marijuana. Noncannabinoids accounted for up to 88% of smoke. These include soot, tars, hydrogen cyanide, carbon monoxide, and a half-dozen polycyclic aromatic compounds (PAHs). PAHs are potent carcinogens.

By contrast, marijuana vapor is up to 95% cannabinoids, plus some terpenes, and one PAH. Vaporization presents the best ratio of tars to cannabinoids as compared to smoking, filtration, or using a water pipe.

Vaporization's efficiency is comparable to smoking up to the point of absorption, where it zooms past combustion. A 2007 studied showed that vaporization results in higher concentrations of THC in plasma, at a faster rate than smoking.

Other studies confirm decreased bronchial irritation from vaping, and irritation is one of the leading side effects of medical marijuana smoking. It can cause bronchitis, which cannabis smokers appear to suffer more of. There's never been a better time to ditch that chronic cough.

The modern vaporizer concept has actually been around for some time. The first known device that worked by vaporizing marijuana was introduced in 1979 under the name the "Tilt Pipe." This short-lived device was doomed to obscurity by the passage of anti-paraphernalia laws in the early 1980s.

In 1994, BC Vaporizers manufactured prototype models of a device and named it the "Vaporizer." The name stuck, and it is now used generically to refer to all of the various vapor devices. Many inventor-types in Europe, Canada, and the United States have emerged since the mid-1990s, flooding the market with choices. This chapter explains how they work and reviews the different types of vaporizers currently available.

HOW VAPORIZERS WORK

Vaporizers capitalize on the fact that THC transforms into a vapor at a lower temperature than the temperature at which plant material burns. Just like water can be turned into vapor, THC resin can be turned from a liquid to a gas without actually combusting the plant material.

Some vaporizers are designed to resemble familiar paraphernalia. There are bong-like models and a few portable types that are similar to pipes. Favorite bongs can even be adapted for vaporization techniques. Other models look like alien gadgetry. All vaporizers involve a heating element, a bowl-like part that holds the marijuana or concentrate, and a way of catching and drawing the vapor.

With the rollback of marijuana prohibition, we're witnessing an explosion in species of desktop, portable, and pocket/pen vaporizers. These devices vaporize raw herb and/or waxy concentrates, oils, and bubble hash and kief.

Patents on the technology have existed since the '60s, but the products began to seep into the consumer consciousness in the mid-2000s, after the Chinese began mass production, which brought costs down dramatically. Am-

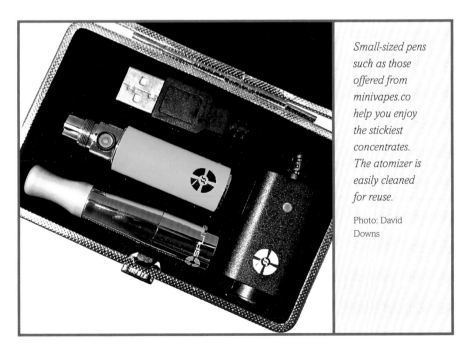

Small-sized pens such as those offered from minivapes.co help you enjoy the stickiest concentrates. The atomizer is easily cleaned for reuse.

Photo: David Downs

plifying consumer adoption was the war on tobacco as well as the rise of medical marijuana. E-cigarettes suddenly became a viable alternative to tobacco smoking, and marijuana-adapted devices became a significant global market.

The Vaporizer High

The first time you use a vaporizer, it may seem odd. You inhale air that has the faintly suggestive odor of cannabis, but there is no smoke. It doesn't quite feel the same. The harshness and flavor of the smoke is noticeably absent. It may even feel like nothing is happening. And then, suddenly, it dawns on you that you're high.

The high may also feel different than when smoking. Some people report that they get stoned quickly when using a vaporizer. Others note that the high seems to be lighter or more head-oriented.

Many people prefer vaporization because its delivery is as rapid as smoking, but without the unwanted tars. Vaporizers and their nicotine counterparts are also not clearly illegal the way using tobacco products are. People are clandestinely vaping everywhere, from City Hall to airports and workplaces. Consequently, laws banning vaporizers in places where smoking is prohibited

Cloud Penz was the first to offer a portable micropen with a micro USB charger. The pens use a lithium ion battery, and the company's atomizers are made with titanium.

Photos: Cloud Penz

are in place all over the country. Critics of such laws are pushing back, noting that there is plenty of scientific evidence that vaping is far safer than smoking, and little evidence that secondhand exposure to exhaled vapor is harmful.

Some smokers adjust easily to vaporization, but others report that the high produced from vaporizing lacks something more than just the smoke. It's important to keep in mind the notion that psychological effects are a function of the drug, the user's mindset, and the overall setting.

Smokers are conditioned to anticipate the high when they taste and feel the smoke. Vaporizing and smoking are both complex chemical exchanges of marijuana's constituents. It seems completely reasonable that they produce subtly different experiences.

Vaporizer Mechanics

A little knowledge helps to ensure an enjoyable and healthy vaporizing experience. There are a few key mechanics that determine a good vaporizer.

The first is heat. Vaporizers are designed to maintain a temperature that is safely within a specific range. THC's boiling point is 392°F (200°C), but non-cannabinoid terpenes vaporize starting at 80°F (27°C). The ideal temperature for vaporization is subject to debate, but is usually suggested in the range 330°F–375°F (165°C–190°C). Smoke begins to form at temperatures over 360°F (182°C). When the temperature goes over the 400°F (204°C) mark, tars and other undesirable compounds such as benzene and dioxins are released. When ignited, the temperature soars to 600°F (316°C) or higher.

Vaporizer heating elements must maintain a stable temperature to produce vapor without burning the plant material. Many vaporizer models are designed to reach the desired temperature range quickly. THC and the other cannabinoids vaporize at slightly different temperatures. Rapid heating delivers the full cannabinoid spectrum simultaneously.

Some vaporizers have temperature control, while others are designed to reach the correct temperature without any adjustable settings. The latter models are convenient because they avoid the learning curve, but they lose flexibility. An adjustable model adds complexity to the process, but contributes to the design. It may take a little experimentation to learn about adjusting the temperature controls.

There are two types of temperature controls: binary (on/off) and analog. The heating element may have settings, allowing the user to monitor the exact temperature. Once the right setting is determined, it only needs occasional, minute adjustments.

Many vaporizer inventors recommend slow, even, meditative breaths for inhaling vapor. Most desktop vapes feature a reservoir or kettle where herb is exposed to heat. When vaporizing, the bowl should expose the greatest possible surface area of the material to the heat source. Greater surface area means more available resin to evaporate. In some units you occasionally redistribute the herb. You can also save the brown, toasted herb waste for use in baking. It still contains some cannabinoids.

With box and whip–style desktop units, moving the reservoir to control the temperature is more intuitive, and involves some coordination while drawing a hit. This may seem like a downside, but it has one advantage: the temperature is determined not only by the heating element, but also by the strength of a person's draw. A strong inhale causes the temperature to fall. After adjusting the heat for such a user, be sure to readjust it for the next person to take a hit.

The bowl should also keep the bud at an even distance from the heat source. Uneven application of heat causes the hotter area to burn or toast, which may produce smoke and alter the taste. The cooler parts will rest in the bowl with the resin intact. Well-designed models have a small vapor collection area. By the time the vapor is inhaled, its temperature has begun to drop. This is better for the lungs, since hot, dry air is unhealthy, even when it doesn't contain smoke. However, as the cannabinoids cool, they condense into liquid dew. Large collection areas provide more surfaces to which the dew can cling, making it irretrievable.

Keep portable and pen vaporizers charged and clean. When purchasing a unit, battery life and ease of loading and cleaning should be chief concerns. Durability and a great warranty are two more key features. On the other hand, some devices are disposable.

Because high temperatures are involved, all materials used to build a vaporizer should be safe when heated. Copper, plastics, aluminum foil, and some other metals release toxic fumes at vaporization temperatures. Models containing these metals create a health hazard and should not be used. Glass, stainless steel, titanium, low-heat-proof formulations of nickel, ceramic, and brass are all safe.

PREPARING HERB FOR VAPORIZING

Bud is sometimes used for vaporizing, but the trend is toward using concentrates. Some devices are designed solely for them. Others require an adapter.

For raw flower–based units, salvaged bud bits work well because the material is ground before it is used. All raw flower–based vaporizers also work with other medicinal herbs.

Grinding the bud improves the flow of air and maximizes the surface area that is exposed to heat. A coarse grind is best. In chamber-type models, kief is easily used by itself. In other models, fine material is layered on top of coarsely ground material to avoid clogging up the works.

Grinder with Strawberry Cough bud.

Photo: Steep Hill Halent

Grinders make quick work of preparing the bud. These pocket-sized disks are filled and twisted to reduce the material. The consistency is determined by the amount of time the material is ground.

Just place the herb inside, join the pieces together, and then twist until the herb is the consistency you want. The pins do the work. These hand-powered grinders let you determine the grind: coarser for pipe smoking, or finer for vaporizing. They work with a variety of herbs, and can also be used to prepare material for other processes, such as kief making.

It is better to use freshly ground buds. Place extra material in an airtight container and store it in a dark, cool place so it doesn't dry out.

One important factor in choosing a grinder is how it feels in your hand. Pick a size that easily enables you to twist it. Size depends on use. Feel free to get a bigger grinder for parties.

Grinders come in a variety of materials that affect how they work. The cheapest are hard plastic grinders, which seize up frequently, feel the chintziest, and make this awful screech. There's also a question of plastic chipping or wearing away in your herb. Wooden grinders with metal pegs work well enough, but the best devices are milled out of solid blocks of superhard aircraft aluminum. Their teeth are precision designed for shredding and they'll outlast the apocalypse. Models with screens on the bottom and a kief-catching chamber are quite popular.

The Vaporizers

All vaporizer models work from the same set of scientific principles. The following descriptions and reviews are intended to give a basic overview of the main types of vaporizers currently available.

The review process has been a group effort. Some vaporizer inventors and designers offered information and review units. We purchased others. We tested each model ourselves for ease of use and quality of results. Then we cross-referenced our findings with public information and reviews from other connoisseurs and experts. Thanks to all who contributed to the development of this chapter.

All prices listed are in U.S. dollars unless otherwise indicated.

VaporBrothers Vapor Box

MSRP: $216.00

Type: desktop, draw

For use in: the home

Use with: flowers

Heating element: ceramic

VaporBrothers Vapor Box Description

VaporBrothers launched the iconic Vapor Box in 1999 and it remains a go-to box and whip–style unit. You load finely ground flowers in the end of the whip, touch it to the hot heating element in the box, and inhale cool vapor. Because this model consists of glass and ceramic heating parts encased in a wood box, you don't have to worry about the parts fuming under heat. Accessories include the VaporBrothers' AromaBulb Oil Diffuser, for use with essential oils. VaporBrothers has also branched out into vape pens with the Dabbler, exclusively for extracts and oils.

VaporBrothers Vapor Box Review

The Vapor Box is about the size of a small brick. It plugs into the wall and has a knob to adjust temperature on it. The whip is Class IV medical-grade plastic tubing that is BPA- and DEHP-free. The Box heats up in under a minute while you grind up some herb in a grinder, and can be left on for long periods

The Vapor Box is a very popular, iconic, desktop whip-style vape.

Photo: VaporBrothers

of time. It takes a little practice to load the end of the whip with the right amount of bud at the right density. You want a fluffy little pinch that fills up about 30% of the end and totally covers the screen.

The Box seems too easy to use. You just hold the herb end of the whip to the heating element on the box and slowly draw on the mouthpiece. Hot air from the element heats up the herb, sending vapor down the tube. You don't want to pull too hard, because all the air will decrease the temperature near the herb and make vaping less effective. The standard whip will give you about four big inhales before the material dries and browns. You'll also need to resituate the herb with the included bamboo pick to fully vape it all. You blow through the tube to expel the spent material into a container. The vapor is thin and white, yet potent, and the effects are subtle. They sneak up on you, compared to a big, hacking bongload. It takes repeated uses with the Vapor Box to fully feel in control of it.

Da Buddha Herbal Vaporizer

MSRP: $190.00

Type: desktop, draw

For use in: the home

Use with: flowers; or oil and waxes, with attachment

Heating element: ceramic

Da Buddha Herbal Vaporizer Description

There are cheaper desktop, whip-style vaporizers out there, but there's no point in buying cheap if you'll never use the thing. Da Buddha's Herbal Vaporizer comes in under $200, and the quality and durability of it ensures it'll be a device you actually use. The base model comes in silver and black, and it looks like a wide cylindrical vase with a broad, flat-foot pad and an open top where the heating element hooks up to the whip. You load grass in the glass tip of the whip and slot it into the connector on the Da Buddha. A knob below, near the bottom, adjusts the temperature of a ceramic heating element which heats up the surrounding air inside the device. When you suck on the whip, the suction pulls the hot air through the cannabis, vaping the THC and sending the vapor down the straw and into your body. Super simple to operate, the Da Buddha represents the entry-level of quality desktop vapes.

Da Buddha Herbal Vaporizer Review

Weighing in at 3.1 pounds, the Da Buddha feels sturdy and comes with a glass kit featuring a heater cover, wand, and mouthpiece, and three feet of tubing. You also get a free padded travel bag, handmade glass marble pick, and free screens for the wand.

Using this thing is as basic as it gets. Finely grind up some herb and use your finger to load a quarter-inch layer into the base of the wand. You want to cover the screen in the base completely with herb, so hot air is forced to flow through the pot, and cannot take the easier way around it. Unless you have some seriously dry, sandy, old herb, you should be able to lightly pack the herb layer and it'll stay caked against the screen, even when it's on its side in the heater cover.

The Da Buddha takes under a minute to heat up and is silent. Just twist the knob to turn it on and set the temp, though you will need to experi-

The Da Buddha is a high-quality, entry-level desktop vape.

Photo: Da Buddha

ment with the temperature gauge to get the desired vapor thickness. (It takes ten minutes at full heat to season the unit on first use, so read the manual while you wait. You can leave the Da Buddha on for extended lengths of time as long as you supervise it. While the outside is harmless, the internal heater and attached glass heater cover do get very hot and you don't want a child or a pet to reach in and touch any of those hot components.)

After the unit is hot and seasoned, it's very simple to use—just attach the wand to the heater cover and draw on the mouthpiece. Cannabinoid vapor will be invisible at first as it travels down the whip to the mouthpiece, but we also saw the telltale white, thin vapor in the hose. Vapor thickness is a function of temperature, how finely ground the material is, how well it's packed, and how hard you suck on the whip. At low temperature and with hard sips you won't see anything at all, though you may get just as stoned as someone blowing fat, milky-white bongloads. At high temperature, with soft little sips, the vapor can get quite thick.

The "Flavor Oil Vapor Kit" is a titanium nail and globe setup custom modified to sit on top of the Da Buddha heating element. Make sure the nail is contacting the Da Buddha heater, turn it up to high, and dab away with high-grade butane hash oil (bubble hash will leave a residue and can burn). It's perfect for folks averse to dabbing with butane torches, or who need a hot nail on standby.

VapirRise

MSRP: $249.99

Type: desktop; forced air

For use in: the home

Use with: flowers; or oils and waxes, with oil cup

Heating element: ceramic, stainless steel

VapirRise Description

Basically the poor man's Volcano, the American-made VapirRise offers all the luxury of a desktop, forced-air vaporizer at about a third of the cost. VapirRise distinguishes itself with a four-way party valve, solvent hash compatibility, and either whip or bag vapor delivery. The downside to all this versatility is that there are about 27 parts in the box, and beginners are going to need an in-person or web tutorial, or to follow the manual to the letter.

VapirRise looks like a pretty, plastic, and futuristic vase, with blue LEDs reminiscent of the SpaceX Dragon orbiter. Where the Germans went wide and bulky with the Volcano, VapirRise went narrow and light, focusing on the central vapor path. On the base, digital touchpads control the temperature and fan, and the unit plugs into the wall, so don't absentmindedly trip over it. It's tempting to get overwhelmed by the companion box of hoses, HEPA filters, valves, clamps, and bags—but don't. Like all vaporizers, it's essentially a glorified hairdryer. Remind yourself of that while you dig for the main pieces.

VapirRise Review

It takes just a few minutes to set up the VapirRise for the first time. You're going to want to plug the device in, grind up some herb, fill the steel herb chamber, snap it onto the steel valve, and affix one of the high-grade heat-resistant plastic tubes (the whip) to the end of the valve. For basic use, start with the whip.

The VapirRise can be used with finely ground cannabis or concentrates.

Photo: Vapir

Set the temperature to 380°F (193°C), hit the heat button, and VapirRise's ceramic heating element will warm up in less than a minute. The fan automatically runs at the 2 setting. When you hit your target temperature, slot the herb chamber into the top and stick the end of the straw in your mouth. VapirRise's quiet little fan forces HEPA-filtered air through the heating element and herb chamber to vaporize the buds. VapirRise blows a soft, lightly scented vapor in your face, so it's incredibly easy to sit back and puff away.

If you're in a group, you're going to want to quickly pass the whip to the next person while the fan is going, so as not to waste vapor. Unfortunately, if you want to turn off the fan while waiting to pass the whip, the heating element also turns off and the temperature starts falling. Turning the heat back up and the fan back on mid-session makes for a few weak hits until the unit gets going again at full temperature. That's where the four-way hookah valve comes in. Slot that four-way splitter on, pack a thicker bowl, and turn the fan and heat up. The VapirRise becomes a vapor fountain for the whole party.

You can switch to a bag instead of the whip, but it requires fitting the bag to the valve. It's sort of like affixing a turkey bag to a banana with a rubber band and a plastic clamp—it takes a few tries to make it look pretty.

Reloading the chamber requires an oven mitt or something else that is heat-proof, and you should never touch any of the steel along the vapor path, which gets very hot. The oil cup performed as advertised with waxes, oil, and shatter, but not as great with bubble hash.

Storz & Bickel Volcano Vaporizer

MSRP: $669.00, Digital with Easy Valve set; $539.00, Classic

Type: desktop; forced air

For use in: the home, medical facilities

Use with: flowers; or oils and waxes, with liquid pad

Heating element: aluminum alloy block

Storz & Bickel Volcano Vaporizer Description

The gold standard in desktop vaporizers is a legitimate medical-grade product manufactured in Tuttlingen, Germany, by medical devices maker Storz & Bickel, and it is featured in some hospitals, as well as many of the best dispensaries. The Volcano gets its name from its conical, brushed metal housing, which looks and feels solidly built at a hefty 3.5 pounds.

The Volcano is the king of forced-air desktop units. These types of vapes push air through the vaporization chamber, instead of requiring the user to suck. The herb chamber sockets into the top of the Volcano and terminates in a heat-resistant, food-grade balloon (like a turkey bag). You control the temperature by adjusting either the dial on the classic version, or setting the temperature with buttons on the digital version. Flick a side switch and the device heats up in as little as three minutes. A second switch turns on the air pump, which forces filtered, heated air through the herb chamber and into the bag, filling it in as little as 90 seconds. Turn off the air pump, disconnect the bag valve, slot on the mouthpiece, and gently inhale. A pressure-sensitive tip keeps the vapor in the bag and only opens when the mouthpiece is pressed to the lips.

Storz & Bickel Volcano Vaporizer Review

The Volcano intimidates and impresses everyone who first meets it. From the heft of the unit to the myriad accessories and components, it's like unpacking alien technology. Thankfully, it's very easy to master.

Loading is easy enough. Use a grinder to finely grind up some herb, and load a thin ($^1/_{16}$" to ½"), even layer of flowers into the bottom of the chamber. Next affix the valve and bag and switch

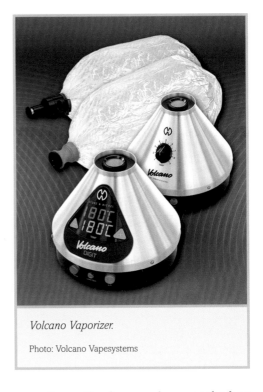

Volcano Vaporizer.

Photo: Volcano Vapesystems

the air pump on to fill it up. You can see the puffs of vapor dance as the bag quickly fills up. The vapor can sit in the bag for hours afterward, but is best consumed fresh.

The trickiest part of the Volcano is the bags, which need to be changed after about 125 sessions. Learning to affix them to the "Solid Valve" takes a few minutes. The manufacturer now sells an "Easy Valve" version with disposable valve-and-bag setup, so when your bag gets dirty, you just toss the whole thing and click on another one.

Volcano's Solid Valve disassembles easily for washing in hot, soapy water, and then in alcohol. Just don't lose track of any of the tiny valve nuts or screens, and follow the manual to reassemble.

The heating chamber gets hot, so use care when emptying spent herb and reloading the chamber. Never touch your fingers to the metal parts. Newer Volcanos come with a liquid pad for use with oils. Similar to a Brillo Pad, the liquid pad provides a nonfuming, metal matrix for the wax to run through and vaporize off of. Instead of placing flowers in the heating chamber you stick the liquid pad in, then some wax, and then the chamber's screen. Note: Do not overload the pad with oil, or vaporize oil in the Volcano without the pad. Both will lead to a messy, gooey cleanup and potential malfunction.

You can readily adjust the vapor quality with the Volcano. Higher heat combined with a thick layer of top-shelf flowers will make for some thick, potent smoke. Lower heat with a small amount of low-potency herb is barely detectable as vapor. Either way, the effects can be profound. Thankfully, the Volcano shuts down automatically after 20 minutes of inattention. Vape bags are about as social as passing around a joint, yet the smoke-free, super-medical styling ensures that the device is used in some hospitals and treatment centers.

Storz & Bickel Plenty

MSRP: $349.00

Type: handheld, plug-in, whip-style

For use in: the home, medical facilities

Use with: raw flowers; or concentrates, with liquid pad

Heating element: 110V, odor-free, food-safe, double helix heat exchanger

Storz & Bickel Plenty Description

Basically a handheld Volcano, the Plenty "Hot Air Generator" delivers powerful medical-grade vape hits without hogging your coffee table with complicated valves and balloons. The size of a large glue gun, it comes with a 12-foot, three-prong cord you need to plug in. The Plenty weighs a pound and a half, and precision heats herb or hash to 266°F (130°C)–396°F (202°C). It features an analog temperature gauge, temperature dial, and on/off switch, as well as an auto-off release handle and temperature fuse to prevent overheating or accidents. The second major component is the herb chamber and stainless steel cooling coil. You draw on a mouthpiece attached to the end of the coil like sucking on a straw. It's very effective, and easy to master.

The Plenty is a hefty, handheld home vape for medical applications.

Photo: David Downs

Storz & Bickel Plenty Review

The design of this thing shouts "German-made medical-grade engineering," down to the quality seal on the box. There are actually very few pieces inside, which is nice. With the six-step, quick-start manual, you can be vaping in about five minutes. The first thing to do is get familiar with the herb chamber, which friction-fits to the cooling coil. Use the included grinder to finely grind up a half-gram of herb and fill the chamber completely and correctly. (The Plenty also comes with a "liquid pad" for vaping wax or smaller amounts of flowers.) Gently screw the chamber onto the cooling coil, and then onto the device body. Plug in and switch on Plenty, then grab the handle to release the auto-off. Set the orange dial to between 5 and 6 and the unit will heat up to around 390°F (199°C) in a few minutes. An orange control light lets you know it's heating up. When the control light turns off with a "flick," you're at the desired temperature. Just grab the handle, stick the mouthpiece in your mouth, and inhale slowly and continually to about half your lung volume, then exhale.

The wide, shallow chamber exposes a huge amount of flower surface area to heat, generating a devilishly thin, tasty, potent vapor that yielded an instant head change for this reviewer. Vapor quality depends on herb quality and quantity, grinding, and how high you set the temp. Because the cooling coil is steel, you cannot see how thick your draw is, so we took some unexpectedly huge hits off the Plenty.

This problem gets even bigger when using the liquid pad. It's really easy to take a very big rip of vaped BHO. (Wax works best, super-runny oils do not.) It takes a session or three to really dial in the device, but it's easy to clean and comes with a three-year warranty—perfect for health-conscious smokers looking for a high-quality, long-lasting (albeit imposing) device for use at home.

Magic Flight Launch Box

MSRP: $119.00

Type: handheld; draw

For use in: anywhere

Use with: flowers; or oils and waxes, with tray

Heating element: stainless steel coil, 2 AA NiMH batteries

Magic Flight Launch Box Description

A cult classic with a rabid online following, the San Diego, CA–made Magic Flight Launch Box is a portable, handheld flower vaporizer that can get a few

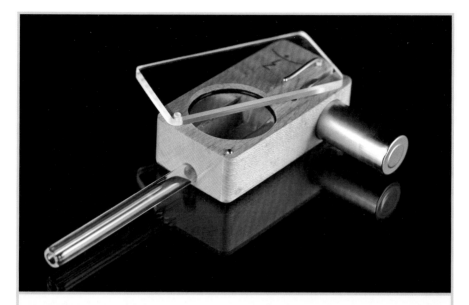

The Magic Flight Launch Box is a quirky but highly effective portable flower vape. Beautiful and practical, these vaporizers are made with the hope that the world will benefit from the love put into each one.

Photo: Magic Flight

people stoned on a single rechargeable AA NiMH battery (though it's best to have backups for parties). The core of the MFLB is a small, light, maple wood block with a plexiglass, swivel-click cover. The cover slides away to reveal a wide cavity lined with a metal screen, where about a half-gram of herb goes. You push a special AA battery into a side port and hold it there to send current through the metal screen, vaporizing cannabinoids by direct conduction, convection, and infrared. Softly sipping the vapor results in astonishingly huge hits and effects, given the ruggedly simple technology involved.

Purportedly developed with the hiker or camper in mind, the Magic Flight Launch Box seems to fit the outdoorsy lifestyle. It achieves elegance through being simple, effective, and natural. Inside its tin travel case, the smooth, light, maple wood block has a familiarity that's lacking from more futuristic vaporizers. It's approachable and friendly looking; it seems to invite you over to pick it up and play with it.

The batteries are "stripped" AAs, meaning the protective plastic "jacket" has been removed from the outside. Stamped with the MFLB logo on the bottom, the custom batteries are capped with black plastic. The caps are there to prevent accidental short circuits. On stripped batteries the entire outside surface is a negative contact. Without the safety cap, these batteries can short in your pocket when a key or coin bridges the tiny gap between the positive anode and the sidewall. Stripped batteries enable the MFLB to make a simple circuit just by inserting one all the way into the box. One reviewer considered the stripped batteries inconvenient at best and possibly a safety hazard. AA batteries are not manufactured for use in "stripped" form.

Magic Flight Launch Box Review

We loaded up our MFLB with some finely ground Jack Herer, inserted one battery, and got no results. The batteries come pre-charged but apparently can go flat as they sit on store shelves. We used the included recharging station on both and were disappointed to note that one battery appeared to be faulty, as its recharge light flashed red and green. It took four hours to fully charge the other battery, but then vaping was as easy as slotting the battery in, counting to five, and softly sipping on the straw. Light, white vapor streamed down the Pyrex and we exhaled a respectable hit. You shake and tap the MFLB to redistribute the herb in the chamber and cook it evenly. Each battery can run for about five straight minutes of vapor draw time. That can work out to one to three bowls, at anywhere from four to 12 draws per bowl, depending on skill. Suffice to say, two fully charged batteries can keep two people baked all day.

It takes seconds to master the art of loading, engaging, and drawing on the MFLB, so the device would be a fabulous unit for someone who's using it once at night before bed. Conversely, the MFLB has the hard-core tokers covered with backup batteries ($7.50 for 2 stripped NiMH AAs), a power adapter for plug-in use, a whip, and a bubbler attachment. (Note: You can buy and strip AA NiMH batteries on your own, but make sure to get 2000 or 2700 mAh. MFLB recommends Maha Powerex 2700s.) MFLB has also made space for concentrates with a small wax tray that you can slot onto the metal screen for vaping oils, waxes, and the like.

One of the best, craziest parts about the MFLB is its "Lifetime Functional Warranty" for any damage or defect. That's right. If you accidentally tear the screen or your dog uses the vape as a chew toy, these San Diego hippies will send you a new one. It's crazy until you realize what's carved on the bottom of MFLB, aside from a serial number: "Love is: that which enables choice; always stronger than fear. Always choose on the basis of love."

It's that positive, optimistic vibe that permeates the MFLB from design to marketing.

Vaped Micro V2 Deluxe/Luxury V2

MSRP: $99.99/$129.99

Type: vape pen

For use in: the home; on the go

Use with: wax (optimal), shatter, oil, or high-grade water extracts (less optimal)

Heating element: titanium coil, wick, battery

Vaped Micro V2 Deluxe/Luxury V2 Description

The award-winning, longtime Bay Area company Vaped has a flourishing line of miniaturized vaporizers for use with wax, other solvent concentrates, and high-grade water extracts. These battery-powered units are similar to their peers in that they pair with a heating element—which Vaped dubs a "skillet bowl"—as well as a mouthpiece. Vaped is also among the first to introduce a "globe" attachment, which is basically a skillet bowl surrounded by a see-through glass chamber that helps pool and cool vapor during use. The globe looks really cool, and is a party pleaser. Vaped's kits also feature some pretty great accessories like a soft, zippered travel case with dabber, different mouthpieces, and even a lanyard so you don't misplace the unit after it has gotten you totally ripped.

The Micro Vaped is an affordable, high-quality wax pen.

Photo: David Downs

Vaped Micro V2 Deluxe/Luxury V2 Review

Vaped immediately distinguishes itself in the crowded pen vape space with its faux-wood, zippered carrying cases. Inside, a dazzling array of interchangeable bits is easily sorted into batteries, "skillet bowls," and mouthpieces. The "globe kit" comes with one globe and two custom-fitted skillet bowls. It takes seconds to learn how to assemble and use either the Micro V2 Deluxe or Luxury V2. First, fully charge the AA-sized batteries in under 30 minutes. A red LED light on the bottom of the Micro will turn off when it's ready. The Luxury V2 has a tiny, LED battery meter at the bottom to tell you when it's full. Screw on a skillet bowl (or a globe), load with wax (or another type of high-grade hash), and then screw on the mouthpiece. The device turns on or off with five quick clicks. Once it's on, press and hold the button for five to 15 seconds while softly inhaling to get a massive rip. You can take about four before the skillet needs a reload, and the battery can go for a couple days.

People absolutely love the globe attachment, because you can watch the white, dense, hash vapor pool in the unit for a few seconds before you take a rip. The visual element is not only exciting; it helps people tightly titrate their dosage. But it's also much less stealthy than the standard skillet bowl, and therein lies the tradeoff. Lower-profile, stealth devices have smaller heating elements and deliver smaller puffs. Bigger units are less stealthy, but can offer bigger hits or features like the globe. You clean the skillet bowl by emptying it out and swabbing it with alcohol-soaked cotton Q-tips. Replacement skillet bowls run $14.99 each or five for $49.99. The steel casing makes this a very, very durable pen vape.

Cloud

MSRP: $59.99

Type: vape pen

For use in: the home; on the go

Use with: wax (optimal), shatter, oil, or high-grade water extracts (less optimal)

Heating element: battery, wick, coil

Cloud Description

State-of-the-art vaporizers are now as small as a common Bic pen, and the leader in the pen vape space is the company Cloud, whose line of tiny, hand-held units for wax and hash have won countless major industry awards. Like many other devices of its miniature size, the Cloud assembles like a teeny, tiny totem pole. A lithium ion battery sits at the bottom. A heating element called an "atomizer" slots into the battery, and a mouthpiece slots onto the atomizer. One button on the front of the Cloud locks and unlocks the device, as well as controls its on/off function. A teensy, red LED on the bottom lights up when the device is charging, and it comes with a wall/USB charger. Using one of these things will blow your mind and change your life.

Cloud Review

Clean, sharp, elegant, innocuous— those are just a few of the words that come to mind as we open up Cloud's iPhone-like white box and hold the extremely lightweight White Cloud in our hands. It looks like a chic, slender tube of lipstick. No one, not even the police, suspects it delivers powerful, mind-altering hits of solvent hash vapor. First we charged the Cloud to full capacity in 30 minutes. After it's charged, you unlock the device by clicking the Cloud button five times fast. It flashes twice to let you know it's on. Then, you season the new atomizer by holding the Cloud button down for ten seconds. The heating element is a wire-wrapped wick run-

The Cloud is an award-winning micropen for concentrates like wax.

Photo: David Downs

ning through the center of a tiny ceramic bowl. Electricity from the battery hits resistance in the coil, causing it to heat up, glow orange, and, of course, vaporize concentrates. Use the included dabber to insert some wax, equivalent to maybe two grains of rice, and make sure to cake it right on the coil. Wax on the edges of the bowl doesn't vape well. Slot the mouthpiece on, hold the pen to your mouth, and softly sip from the tip while holding the Cloud button for 5–15 seconds. The Cloud delivers big, medium-bodied hits of hash equivalent to a 10-inch bongload. Used with good wax, the Cloud's soft, light, flavorful vapor goes down smooth yet packs a wallop. The tiny chamber makes it best for a couple of quick personal hits on the go, but it's also very easy to reload for party bowls. The powerful battery withstood three days of heavy use at a bachelor party on two charges. The atomizer lasts no longer than 90 days and costs $14.99 to replace. The Cloud opens up a whole new world of places to get stoned.

Grenco Science microG

MSRP: $99.95

Type: micro vape pen

For use in: anywhere

Use with: medium-to-thick essential oils, shatter, wax, honeycomb, or high-grade bubble hash

Heating element: steel alloy

Grenco Science microG Description

Another extremely stealthy, well-made unit, Grenco Science's current generation microG pen comes with a host of upgrades over the original, highly successful microG. Chief among them is what they call the "microG tank." That's the part that gets hot and vaporizes concentrates. The new microG comes with four stainless steel tanks, each containing a metal coil that heats up when electric current passes through it. Each one screws onto the battery unit, which is an innovation over the older method of squeeze-holding the tank against the battery by way of a rubber gasket. The new microG tanks and battery unit thread easily and tightly, and the entire device feels more solid than your average vape pen. The black mouthpiece slides down over the tank, and the kit comes with five mouthpiece sleeves for sharing. The microG recharges through a mini firewire connection and comes with a USB adapter as well as a wall adapter. Rounding out the kit is a microG tool on a keychain, two glass containers for holding wax, and some alcohol-soaked "G Tips" for cleaning the tanks.

Grenco Science microG Review

This is another game changer of a device that is going to become the default mode of consuming cannabinoids for a whole different set of people than your stereotypical stoners.

There's nothing about the thin, small device that screams "weed." Professional working women can stow a microG in their purses and innocuously vape at lunch. The sweet light vapor dissipates immediately into the air, and doesn't smell like pot. The black, hard yet grippy cover feels like it won't slip out of your hand, but the stainless steel underneath makes it feel solid and well built.

The microG is an award-winning wax-only micropen.

Photo: David Downs

We charged the device for two to three hours for the first couple uses, and a red LED on the bottom turns off when the battery is full. Unlike other vape pens, the microG automatically shuts down charging when the battery is full, so you don't have to worry about forgetting, overcharging, and ruining the pen.

The device features a lock/unlock mechanism so you don't accidentally turn it on in your pocket. Click the steel "micro" button five times fast to disengage the lock. At first, we ran the microG dry just to see how the steel coil performed. It quickly got red hot, without sizzling, popping, or fuming—exactly what you want to see in such devices.

The microG excels at vaping honeycomb, shatter, medium-to-thick oil, and high-grade bubble hash. We'd avoid using low-grade bubble hash because the residue in it will stick to the inside of the tank and degrade the coil faster. (Coils last about four to six weeks depending on use and cost $14.95 to replace.)

After loading up the tank with a tenth of a gram of high-grade hash, we pressed and held the "micro" button for 10 seconds while we softly drew air from the mouthpiece. If you listen closely you can hear the coil vaping the hash with a sizzle. The microG generates a thin, narrow stream of vapor that you can hardly tell you are inhaling. But when you exhale, out comes this large-sized vapor hit. One puff should be enough for most people, and each tank can hold maybe four or five hits' worth before you need to refill. It takes some practice to get deft at loading the tiny tank with the precious hash, but in a day we got good enough to do it in the dark at concerts.

The downside is that great concentrates are not nearly as prevalent as flowers, and you can't use the microG with flowers. Grenco Science makes a version of the microG for flowers, as well as larger-sized units that feature a steel tank that you pack with herb. A heating element inside the tank toasts the herb.

The microG kit offers some of the most bang for your buck in terms of tanks, chargers, containers, and cleaning equipment. (You'll want to clean the tank with the alcohol-soaked "G Tips" to remove any residue around the threads and battery connection. Don't swab inside the tank. It's too sticky; you'll clog the tank with cotton. Also, don't steep any microG components in alcohol. You'll damage them.)

By far the best accessory you can get is the microG travel case, which is the size of a cigarette case and molded to fit the battery, tank, and mouthpiece, and comes with a tiny USB charger. A loaded microG case with a gram or two of CO_2 honeycomb is literally all you need for a two-week vacation. Electrical parts come with a one-year warranty.

Vaporite Sapphire

MSRP: $49.99

Type: vape pen

For use in: the home; on the go

Use with: semifluid oils

Heating element: battery, wick, steel coil

Vaporite Sapphire Description

A key member of the vape pen family is "oil tank"–style devices that work with semifluid cannabis oil like BHO or CO_2 extracts. These amber-colored, potent oils are sold at major dispensaries in the United States and must be poured into the oil tank. The Vaporite Sapphire vaporizes your oils and e-juices using a convection current generated by the Sapphire's "clearomizer," or oil tank. Vaporite has been focusing on affordable vaporizers for over ten years, and the reasonable $49.99 unit comes in black, blue, red, green, and silver. Like many in its class, it features a rechargeable lithium ion battery, which screws onto the oil tank, which in turn screws into the mouthpiece. You unscrew the mouthpiece to dribble oil in and refill the tank, which holds up to 1.6 mL of THC oil or e-juice. The Sapphire measures five inches tall and a half-inch in diameter, and since it looks just like an e-cigarette, it is very stealthy.

Vaporite Sapphire Review

In a crowded field of oil tank–style vape pens, the Sapphire stands out as especially easy to reload. A lot of pen vapes require several steps of disassembly to refill, but with the Sapphire, you just unscrew the mouthpiece and load it up. You'll have a harder time finding oil that's the right viscosity to flow into the Sapphire.

You want something runny enough that it can be squirted, or funneled into the tank, but thick enough that it won't leak when the pen is accidentally inverted.

We had to put our syringe of THC refill oil in a Ziploc bag and place it in hot water to warm it up enough to flow into the tank, and even then it wanted to gunk up the top rim instead of flowing down into the bottom of the tank. A little more time warming in the baggy and some centripetal force got things down to where we wanted them to be. Inside the tank, two wicks soak up the oil and transfer it through osmosis into the tank's central heating area.

Click the power button five times rapidly to unlock the battery, and the LED light on the bottom of the Sapphire will flash a few times. Then simply place your lips on the mouthpiece, press down on the power button while inhaling gently for about five seconds, release the button, and exhale. (The device's auto-shut-off kicks in after 12 seconds of power.)

You can see thin vapor fill the empty space in the tank, which is a great form of visual feedback. We were very satisfied with the size of the vapor hits we could get off the Sapphire, as well as how smooth, cool, and light the vapor was without sacrificing potency at all.

The Vaporite Sapphire is an inexpensive oil tank–style vape pen.

Photo: David Downs

The lithium ion battery has more than enough power to keep the average person stoned on hash oil all day. It recharges in two to three hours via USB (with or without an AC adapter). The Sapphire is smart enough to auto-sleep after three minutes without use. The battery lasts about 300 charges, and replacements are cheap.

Bottom line, the Sapphire is a dirt-cheap, medium-quality, oil-tank vape pen that we love to have in our toolkit.

Vaporite Emerald

MSRP: $99.99

Type: vape pen

For use in: the home; on the go

Use with: flowers

Heating element: ceramic oven, stainless steel coil

Vaporite Emerald Description

The Vaporite Emerald is part of a line of pens for flowers (Emerald), waxes (Ruby), and oils (Sapphire) carried exclusively at VaporNation.com. A solid, accessibly priced, stealthy pen vape that takes flowers, the Vaporite Emerald really typifies a subset of the pen market. It costs under $100, is the size of a large pen or highlighter, and comes in black, green, silver, or blue. It's lithium ion battery–operated and rechargeable, and vapes (or sometimes burns) flowers by way of a stainless steel coil inside a ceramic chamber. The exterior is rubber-cased

The Vaporite Emerald is a mid-level flower pen.

Photo: David Downs

steel, with an LED light on the bottom and another on the center button. You charge the device via USB with or without an AC adapter, and you turn it on or off with five swift clicks to the center button.

Vaporite Emerald Review

The Vaporite Emerald isn't meant to last through the years, but at $89.99 with online discounts, you can afford to burn through one each year. It has a paltry, 90-day warranty on the battery, but that's typical for this class, which all seems to come out of the same factory in China, with different labels. The technology involved isn't rocket science, and competition has brought prices down.

A rocket is a good way to think of the Emerald. The components stack on top of one another like an old rocket, with the battery at the bottom, followed by the herb chamber, connector, filter, and mouthpiece. The Emerald uses standard 510 threading so it can pair with other accessories that do as well. The trickiest part of the Emerald is the tiny, disposable ceramic screens. They have to be inserted in the herb chamber at the bottom against the heating coil so they can act as a buffer that keeps the red-hot coil from directly contacting and burning the flower.

We first tried to use the Emerald without the ceramic screen and got a smoky thick hit equivalent to puffing on a joint. We also blackened the inside of the heating chamber. D'oh.

But with the ceramic screen in there, the Emerald actually works as a decent vaporizer, delivering light, sweet, potent vapor hits. The device came out of the box with a charge, and we were vaping in seconds with two to three pinches of herb in the chamber. Just hold the center button down for a few seconds and softly inhale the vapor. The device automatically shuts off if held for longer than 12 seconds, and auto-sleeps if not used for three minutes. It takes 2–3 hours to recharge the battery, which is good all day. The battery lasts about 300 charges, and Vaporite parts are among the cheapest to replace, which is good because the ceramic heating chamber only lasts for about a month of regular use. Cleaning after every use with the included brush prolongs the oven's life-span.

This thing is stealthy! It looks like any other e-cig, and so long as you blow vapor and not smoke, no one in public is the wiser. For a middle-of-the-road flower pen vape, we were very satisfied.

Ploom Pax

MSRP: $249.99

Type: portable

For use in: the home; on the go

Use with: flowers; plus high-grade bubble hash and/or kief

Heating element: nonceramic tuned thin film; stainless steel

Ploom Pax Description

The reigning champ of portable flower vapes is the Pax, designed in San Francisco by Ploom and manufactured oversees.

It's a high-quality, long-lasting, chic device, about the size of a squat flashlight, that easily fits in your palm. The Ploom Pax is a conduction vape, with a tiny oven in the bottom hooked up to a built-in, quick-recharge battery. It's officially for use with tobacco, but its compatibility with pot is widely known.

Finely ground herb goes into the oven in the bottom, which is secured by a magnetized plug. You click the rubber mouthpiece on top to turn on the Pax, and it heats up in seconds. A tiny little LED on the body goes green when it is ready. Softly drawing on the mouthpiece delivers ample vapor hits. The Pax has three temperature settings, which are adjusted by a switch hidden in the bottom. It comes in green, blue, purple, and black, with a 10-year warranty on defects.

Ploom Pax Review

The Pax makes its case for quality right from the simple, minimal packaging. It comes with a small charging dock, instruction manual, and cleaning brush. It's weighty at 2.6 oz, and it feels solid. The outer shell is bead-blasted anodized aluminum, like an Apple MacBook, so it's built to withstand the inevitable drop. All plastic components are food-safe engineering plastics, and the vapor path is constructed entirely from medical-grade components.

We love how smart this thing is. The lithium ion internal battery charges in its dock in under two hours. The Pax has smart-charge technology, so the device can be charged in any state—full or empty—and cannot be overcharged. It also has an onboard accelerometer, so if it sits still for 20 seconds, it goes into standby mode and lowers the oven's heat to 302°F (150°C). If it sits still for three minutes, it shuts off. You can also shake the Pax to check the battery life. The four tiny LEDs flash green when full, or glow red when drained.

The Pax represents the high end of the portable flower vape market.

Photo: Ploom

The Pax's three settings are low (370°F [188°C]), medium (390°F [199°C]), and high (410°F [210°C]). We recommend setting it to medium to start. The oven in the bottom can fit about three-quarters of a gram, and you'll want to fill it up halfway or more. (It's a conduction vaporizer, so the heat is transferring off the walls of the steel box onto the plant matter.)

The two neodymium magnets that secure the oven plug are incredibly strong and sub-flush with the housing, so you don't have to worry about it popping off in your pocket.

The Pax heats up rapidly, in under 30 seconds, and drawing softly yields a thin, flavorful vapor. You're not going to get fat, thick hits off the Pax—it's not that kind of device. But the vapor is just as potent. A fully charged Pax will last one medium-level smoker for about one day of use. Heavy tokers wish it lasted longer. But you can also mix in some high-grade bubble hash or kief for stronger hits. Use hash that's going to leave very little residue, and don't use any oil or BHO. When it gets hot, BHO liquefies and goops things up. You clean the Pax with the included brush every dozen or so uses, and it also comes with a packet of mouthpiece lubricant, if you find the on/off switch sticking.

Our biggest complaint is the lack of visual feedback when hitting the Pax. Actually seeing the vapor or smoke is such an intrinsic part of smoking or vaping, and is crucial to titration. Sipping on the Pax provides no such information. Only the taste, temperature, and lung-feel of the vapor gives you any clue as to how big a hit you took—until you exhale, and by then it's too late. The Pax is also less stealthy than some of its competitors. But those are minor issues. The Pax is a luxury item for dedicated connoisseurs, and neophytes love it, too.

*Nectar Collector's Rocket Girl
by Laceface, Raven Johnson,
and Kristian Merwin.*

Photo: Wasatch Glassworks

Chapter 6.

Dabbing—
The Gear

Accessories for consuming marijuana concentrates are as old as the substances themselves, which go back for thousands of years, but consumers today are witnessing an explosion in dab gear with more products hitting the market every day.

This honeycomb has ideal dryness and a great, light color.

Photo: David Downs

Dabbing is the act of vaporizing concentrated cannabis. Most often people use special pipes designed or modified to consume concentrated cannabis products. The term "dabbing" presumably comes from the tiny amount ("dab") of concentrate needed for a single dose.

Dabbing is a way to consume large amounts of THC and other cannabinoids with radically less smoke. For example, patients with Crohn's disease or

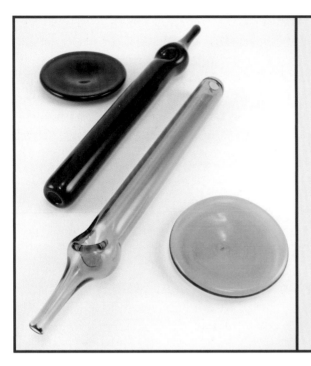

multiple sclerosis can use one dab instead of smoking an entire joint in order to get the same relief from stomach pain or muscle spasms, respectively.

The Kiss Shatter.

Photo: Mel Frank

Marijuana concentrates offer potent levels of cannabinoids and intense medicinal or recreational effects, with just a fraction of the vapor or smoke volume and attendant irritation of raw cannabis. Modern marijuana averages 12% THC in the raw flowers, but modern concentrates can be four to six times that potent. Instead of smoking a joint, dabbers enjoy just a tiny sip of flavorful, cool, ultrapotent hash vapor.

Dabbing is to marijuana what hard liquor shots are to beer. In addition to having clear medical applications, dabs are used by recreational smokers for many of the same reasons: They offer powerful effects with less smoke. Dabs get you very stoned, very quickly.

Since 2009, concentrates have surged in popularity in the medical marijuana epicenters and have been spreading to others. Dispensaries that once carried a shelf of water hash now have three shelves of concentrates. At marijuana festivals, the once-ubiquitous vapor bag for large groups had nearly disappeared by 2014, replaced by an oily dab rig and bud tenders doling out dab after dab to an endless line of enthusiasts.

"THE CLEAR" CONCENTRATE

A concentrate so pristine, "clear" is in the name, The Clear first began appearing in Bay Area dispensaries in 2013 and has since shot to the front of the class. The Clear is an ultra-refined, very viscous, oil-like concentrate that is transparent with gold or yellow tints.

The Clear is used in vape pens or as dabs, because the product tests at 75%–80% THC. It smells sweet and hits incredibly smoothly with immediate effects. It also comes in a number of strains: Jack Herer, True OG, Trainwreck, and Headband.

The pure quality and high percentage of THC in The Clear means that you can eat it, but the raw taste is unpalatable. However, its evanescent flavor profile is ideal for hyper-potent edibles that don't taste weedy. It's already been decarboxylated, so don't worry about that step. Just dilute it in oil or alcohol.

The Clear creation process is proprietary, but the manufacturer says that the process involves heat and pressure. It claims that no residual solvent is detected at the parts-per-billion scale. The company says that it captures the terpenes, decarboxylates the extract to activate it, and then returns the captured terpenes to the mix.

The painstaking process is both the advantage and the drawback. By removing and re-adding terpenes, The Clear tastes like a next-gen extract, with very little of the nose of high-quality bubble hash or BHO. Very much akin to CO_2 extract, the thin smell makes sense after the intense extraction and decarboxylation process. It's also very sticky and tacky at room temperature, yet liquid under heat—so it doesn't work well alone in a normal pipe. Paired with a vape pen or an oil rig, The Clear is among the most potent, clean hits in weed history.

Photo: Nadim Sabella Photography

Sitting safely to dab.

Photo: Saucey Santos

Accessories for using concentrates are specifically adapted to the special properties of hash. Marijuana concentrates don't vaporize or burn like raw flowers. Bubble hash can catch fire, or melt down into a bowl. Solvent hash of all kinds turns to a liquid under heat and coats the sides of a standard pipe. You need special tools to consume such products safely and efficiently.

That usually starts with a globe and nail, also called a dome and nail. The two pieces affix to the downstem of standardized borosilicate tubes (bongs) and bubblers. Newer nails don't require the dome, and the nail

HBC WAX

HBC is a solvent-free wax made, as the name describes, in a hyperbaric chamber. What was once only used for decompressing divers and oxygen therapies for the ill is now creating wax with clean and delicious terpene profiles. Similar to other wax-making processes HBC uses cool temperatures to remove cannabinoids. Hyperbarometric pressure with a reverse nitrogen boil work to pull the cannabinoids and terpenes off of plant matter. Once liquid, the concentrate is filtered through several filters sorting trichomes by density, and then is turned to wax by reversing

Photo: Nadim Sabella Photography

pressure several atmospheres. This process retains both lower and higher level terpenes and produces a product that is fragrant as well as potent. For some there is no going back to solvent concentrates and this is the only item they look for, often coming up empty handed due to still very low volumes on the market.

"HBC tastes and smells stronger than any other wax. People are often surprised the first time they inhale it because there is such a huge difference in the amount of flavor you experience. When dabbed, it feels less hot than expected, and you notice the effects immediately as you exhale. It melts down nicely, leaving little to no residue. HBC is the only thing on the market comparable to Clear when it comes to THC levels and solventless concentrates." —HBC Wax enthusiast

has been eliminated in some versions in favor of a bowl with a shallow outer moat that holds the concentrate as it vaporizers. Tiny holes allow the vapor to be drawn into the tube. These pieces also pair with "dab rigs," which are bubblers of varying sizes that are specially designed for use with hash.

Nails require a heat source to achieve surface temperatures suitable for vaporizing hash. The choices are external, using a small butane torch, or internal, heating the shallow bowl electrically. Skillets, also called swings, which fit into a bong or bubbler, are less popular. Health stones are porous, inert ceramic rocks or puffed glass that fit into specially designed pipes. Waxes and oils are temporarily trapped in the structure as they melt so they can be easily vaped.

DAB GEAR

Nails

Nails are the workhorse of the dab world. They get their name because they look like a standard construction nail: they're long, thin metal objects that fit into a bong's downstem on one side, with a wider top section for vaping hash. They come in a variety of standard widths, like 10 mm, 14 mm, and 18 mm, to fit into different downstems. Nails are made from a variety of materials that are used because they do not create fumes at working vaporization temperatures. The most common materials used are quartz, titanium, and ceramic.

You heat up the nail with a torch, which is usually a six-inch or larger butane torch, with flame control, a safety lock, and a flame lock. Affix the nail in the downstem (wide side up), flick on and lock the torch, and touch the flame

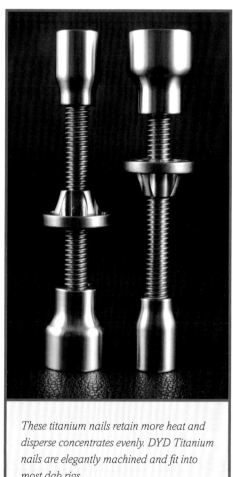

These titanium nails retain more heat and disperse concentrates evenly. DYD Titanium nails are elegantly machined and fit into most dab rigs.

Pipes for the connoisseur of glass, these JAG x Hitman collaborations use various scientific filtration methods for a unique experience.

Photo: Hitman Glass

to the nail. Inhaling air that has been superheated by a nail is not healthful, so most dabbers are attached to water pipes that cool the vapor. Remove the torch as the nail shows the first faint signs of glowing, then place the dab on the nail. The dab flash-melts and boils, generating vapor. Inhale.

A quartz nail inside a Pyrex dome. Nails are heated until they are hot enough to vaporize concentrates.

Photo: David Downs

Nails come in two main varieties, domed and domeless. The dome helps corral the hash vapor and force it down the stem, but it requires that you place it onto the hot nail, which is an extra step. Domes can also get quite arty and beautiful. Domeless nails contain holes in the nail and other design tweaks to force the vapor down during inhalation and prevent it from escaping into the room.

A dome cap makes the rig more efficient. It is placed over the dome immediately after the dab has been dropped on the nail. It prevents the vapor from escaping from the dome

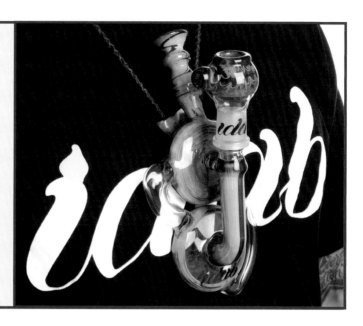

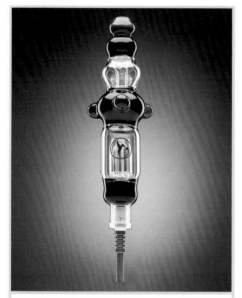

This handheld vertical vaporizer is a spill-proof double bubbler. Heat the glass tip and dip into an extract. Nectar Collectors clean and cool the vapor while allowing you to control both heat and dosage.

Photo: Wasatch Glassworks

top and slows any burning by making oxygen scarce in the dome.

Dabbing Rigs

While nails are designed to fit into a wide variety of downstems, they often fit the best with "dab rigs," bongs, and bubblers specially designed for consuming hash.

Dab rigs tend to be smaller than water pipes for flowers. Since hash smoke is so much more potent, you don't need to fill a huge chamber with smoke to achieve the desired highness. The length of the system is actually a liability here, as solvent hash condenses along the route of delivery. The longer the route, the more condensation, and hence, waste.

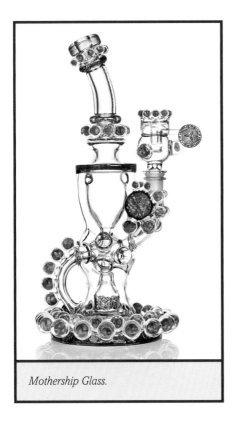

Mothership Glass.

Consequently, dab rigs tend to closely resemble traditional, hand-held bubblers.

Dab rig design is divided into two general classes, "scientific" and "heady," though plenty of artists seek to fuse the two. Scientific designs hew toward a minimalist, lab aesthetic and often feature clear glass and shapes that evoke beakers and test tubes. Form follows function in scientific glass. "Heady" dab rig designs embrace the imagination, taking on the shape of mythic creatures and pushing the boundaries of color, pattern, and materials.

At the larger end of the scientific dab rigs are units like the Sheldon Black medium rig with Ti nail. Fourteen inches tall, sleek and minimal, the Sheldon Black downstem ends in a diffuser, which helps cool and filter the vapor. Scientific dab rigs can get incredibly technical, with multiple levels of diffusers and percolators.

Heady dab rigs vary just as much in size and shape, but the trend is toward smaller rigs. Pendant rigs that fit on a necklace are popular. Heady designers are in a permanent arms race for the newest glass colors and coolest-looking designs and materials. Dragons, robots, cartoon characters, and monsters abound. Designers regularly use metallic fuming to bind different elements to the borosilicate glass, creating deep, rich, luminous colors, sparkles, and interference patterns. Mothership Glass offers some of the most intricate designs, and artists like Snic are pushing the envelope, incorporating external electroplating for steampunk-like designs. The artists designing these rigs are creating a new genre of art that will be used in daily life, but also saved as collectibles.

Electric Dabbers

Many people are turned off by the butane torch, which looks so industrial and primitive at the same time. Electric dabbers heat a nail or stage without using a flame. Companies offer plug-in electric heating elements that affix to a nail and heat it up in seconds.

Handheld electric wands such as Embur or Phedor function on the same principle, using electrical resistance to heat the tip to red hot, which can be applied to instantly vaporize hash on a cold nail.

Health Stone Glass features the Vapor Stone, a ceramic insert that holds concentrates so they are easily vaporized in its labyrinth of cells.

Photo: David Downs

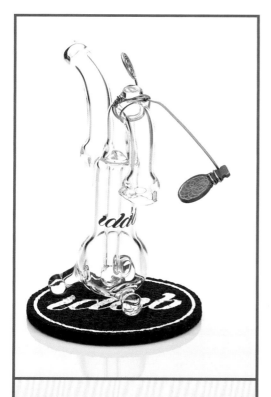

Skillet rigs are easy to use and do not need attachments to vaporize. Dabbing with a skillet from idab's glass line is easy; just heat and swing it under the opening, add concentrate, and enjoy. No nail required.

Health Stones

By far the simplest, easiest way to smoke solvent hash harkens back to using a handheld pipe. With a health stone, the bowl is fitted with what looks like a rock. Vapor stones are 100% inert ceramic rock, so they don't fume. Under heat, solvent hash melts into and vapes out of the porous, rocky matrix. The company Health Stone started in California in 2010, and makes the stones, as well as the glass pipes and bong fittings they go into.

Skillets (Swings)

Skillets, also known as swings, are tiny titanium pans the size of a postage stamp, held below a vapor intake by a metal wire (the "swing" part). You heat up the skillet with a torch, swing

This electric dichro flower petal dish and dabber from piper GingerELA lends a feminine elegance to a dab session. Dip inside for a morsel of nectar.

Photo: David Downs

it under the nozzle, then dab the hash on the skillet while inhaling. Skillets come as attachments for bongs and bubblers, or as part of heady dab rigs.

Wands (Dabbers)

Working with concentrates can get very sticky. They range in texture from granular, sand-like bubble hash to some of the stickiest tree sap imaginable. Nonstick surfaces, usually parchment paper or silicone (not wax paper, which transfers wax and will make your hash taste like a candle), are used to store and transport concentrates. Dabbers are used to manipulate the material, titrate dosage, and apply hash directly to hot surfaces.

All dabbers must be able to withstand high heat without generating fumes. The most popular materials for dabbers are titanium and quartz. Sometimes dabbers look as cruel and utilitarian as a dental pick, or a thimble with a flat-head extrusion. But dabbers and the dishes they come with are often treated as works of art in their own right, and can cost hundreds of dollars. Quartz dabbers are made to look like Bic pens and yellow #2 pencils. Dabbers and dishes often tie in thematically to dab rigs to create visual harmony and lend self-expression to the ritual.

Wish your dab tools wouldn't roll away? Square, ergonomic tools from Mystic Timber are handcrafted using wood from sustainable forests.

Photo: Mystic Timber

Nothing sticks to NoGoo silicone containers and trays. They are a must for storing and transporting concentrates since they eliminate the mess and loss of material to other containers.

Photo: NoGoo

DANGERS OF DABBING

Dabbing has an inherently dangerous look to it, and that may be part of the attraction for some dabbers. Butane torches put people off, as do the red-hot nails, and the sight of strange-looking substances boiling off into glassware. Many people consider dab culture a liability to the overall legalization of marijuana, noting how the media have dubbed it "the crack" of pot. The analogy is incorrect. Dabs are more like the espresso or hard liquor of pot.

Unlike liquor, there is no lethal dose for marijuana. However, you can pass out from flowers or a dab. THC lowers blood pressure, so dab sitting down. Overdosing on THC, while not toxic, can be uncomfortable, causing anxiety and even nausea. Don't dab unless you're an experienced marijuana user. Even then, dabs aren't a contest. Do small dabs and enjoy yourself. Huge dabs increase your tolerance, can result in acute intoxication, and can be part of a constellation of behaviors that could ultimately lead to harm. Keep temperatures as low as possible to vaporize extracts. Sudden exposure to very hot, dry air can cause your throat to close up, as though you were choking. Prevent any physiological damage to your lungs and throat by using a pipe cooled with water or ice.

And of course, use care and common sense when operating a torch, as well as handling potentially hot nails, wands, etc.

DYD Titanium

Company Spotlight

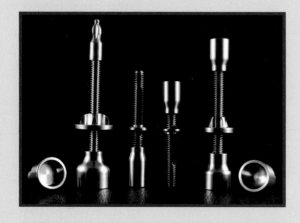

As enthusiasts and patients have turned to the potent, purified concentrates that have become more widely available, specialty companies have emerged with purpose-built products for smoking or vaporizing them. Today's connoisseurs prefer special rigs designed to make the most of small amounts of concentrate, minimizing waste and maximizing flavors and effects. That's where DYD Titanium comes in.

DYD Titanium's signature product is the dabbing nail, machined in the United States from domestic Grade 2 titanium for superior heat retention and performance. Titanium is inert, making it safe to handle the temperatures required to vaporize concentrate. Since the Northern California company was founded in 2010, they have refined their design to precisely sculpted nails that easily adapt to different rigs. DYD Titanium chooses its material for both form as well as function—together, these provide an aesthetically and physically beautiful experience.

Each of their adjustable nails features a goblet-like head cup with thin, machined walls for rapid heat-up, and a thick base that maximizes heat retention. The innovative counterweight does more than keep the nail upright in the rig. It is a machined 9 mm head in its own right, quick heating and perfect for catching smaller dabs of oil.

The slim threaded shaft of the midsection also differentiates the DYD Titanium design. Its narrow diameter allows superior airflow, and the threaded, finned 18 mm midsection adjuster lets you position the nail head at exactly the right height for any rig.

DYD Titanium offers unique tools designed and engineered in collaboration with local artists. The company thoroughly inspects and hand polishes every piece before it's shipped, and takes pride in the fact that everything offered is made in the USA. DYD Titanium's nails can be found in hundreds of stores throughout the United States, Canada, Germany, France, and Japan.

Mothership Glass

Company Spotlight

Some of the world's most innovative borosilicate glass art comes out of Mothership Glass, launched in 2012 as a collaboration between Scott Deppe and Jake Colito. The two have carefully selected more than a dozen skilled artisans to work at their facility in Bellingham, Washington, where the emphasis is on exploring new processes and techniques made possible by state-of-the-art equipment.

Deppe and Colito have a combined experience of more than 25 years on the torch, but they put two years into research and development of scientific glassblowing, perfecting the company's unique percolation system before they turned to color and pattern work. That paid off their first year, with two awards at the American Glass Expo, the industry's largest trade show.

Their products are as functional as they are artistic. Many pieces reflect sacred geometry in their percolation and diffusion systems. The designs, which take anywhere from 12–18 hours of work to construct, have made Mothership Glass an industry leader, backed up by superior customer service and a no-flaw guarantee. Careful work makes it possible. Some parts have tolerances as tight as 0.25 millimeter, and even the logo etching is deep and distinctive. Every piece passes through the hands of 9–12 artisans on average.

As concentrates became popular, Mothership Glass debuted its honeypot design. It uses a free-moving swing arm with either a titanium or quartz bucket, eliminating sticky joints from the rig. Just heat up the bucket away from the bowl and then swing it inside. The D-cut on the bucket creates even air flow. The OFZ cap accessory adapts it for vaporizing.

Mothership Glass's commitment to community comes through in not just their approach to work but their philanthropy. They regularly donate pieces to events that benefit charitable causes, including the Evergreen State Project.

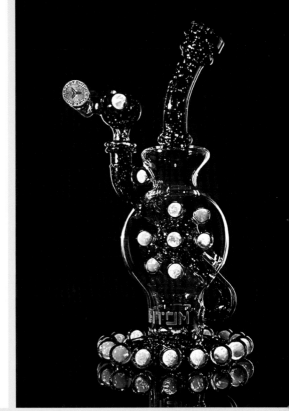

Health Stone Glass

Company Spotlight

The revolutionary Health Stone system, available in many glassware styles from vapor slides to fully worked collaborations, has its proprietary Vapor Stones at the center. Unlike other concentrate tools, the Vapor Stone allows you to take hits of concentrates much like taking a hit of a bowl.

Vapor Stones are small, manufactured discs with a texture similar to pumice whose tiny gaps capture essential oils. When you heat the center of the stone, the oils become viscous and absorb, vaporizing out of its pores. Vapor Stones are inert, made to tolerances of under $1/1000$ of an inch, and are easily replaced in whatever rig you're using. The materials and manufacture are all 100% U.S.

With no loss of oil or vapor, $1/100$ of a gram of concentrate can provide a hit when used properly. The efficiency and convenience of the Vapor Stone and the smooth, milky quality of its hits have made it the go-to piece for numerous aficionados.

The "health" in the company name comes not only from the benefits of the essential oil vapor compared to smoke, but also the heating method. Using a quick flame from the recommended triple-flame cigar torch is less damaging to the environment than using the larger torches commonly used to heat other utensils.

The idea for Vapor Stones came in 2004 when Chad Soren, the founder of Health Stone Glass, was introduced to concentrates that were completely vaporizable, leaving no ash at all. There were many challenges in creating the Vapor Stone, but through determination and a refusal to compromise, he eventually achieved success.

Since 2009, the California-based company has grown into an operation with an office in the San Diego area and two production facilities with 16 workers. Sales have continued to increase every year, and there are plans to expand.

BHO Honeycomb.

Photo: Steep Hill Halent

Chapter 7.

Butane Extracts—

Making BHO Budder, Shatter, Wax

The popularity of products made using butane—hash oil, wax, budder, and shatter—is surging for a number of reasons. They include the products' strength, versatility in vape pens, and their potential as purer, healthier ways to inhale THC and other cannabinoids. Their THC content is often over 80%, compared to an average of 15% THC for high-grade raw marijuana. Using concentrates is healthier than smoking raw buds, since butane hash oil (BHO) contains no vegetative material and few tars or other carcinogens. The extraction process also kills bacteria, mold, and fungi present in the source material.

Processors prefer butane for a number of reasons: it's inexpensive and easy to obtain, the equipment is relatively inexpensive, and it has a good extraction efficiency.

OG Kush supermelt.

Photo: Nadim Sabella Photography

These techniques use butane to dissolve marijuana's active ingredients, cannabinoids, and terpenes from the plant matter. Then the solvent is evaporated, leaving the resin. This can be refined further into a number of products.

Butane extraction is by far the most popular chemical extraction method for marijuana because it's the cheapest technique available. Inexpensive equipment can be used to refine low-grade trim—though *Beyond Buds* adamantly advises against it. Butane extraction is an industrial process best suited to professionals.

Honey Bee Glass Extractors are easy to use and great for first timers who need a dependable unit that seals well and cleans up nicely.

Photo: Honey Bee

HOW BLASTING WORKS

Under magnification, the glands, also called trichomes, look like tiny, clear, white, or amber mushrooms sticking up from the leaf tissue. They consist of a waxy membrane that holds the active ingredients in marijuana—THC and other cannabinoids—as well as aroma molecules called terpenes.

The oils in the trichomes are hydrophobic, meaning they do not dissolve in water the way sugar or salt does. However, the oils dissolve in solvents such as butane and alcohol.

Once all the trichomes are dissolved and removed from the plant, the waste is thrown away and the extract is purged of its solvent, leaving concentrated cannabinoids behind.

DANGERS AND ENVIRONMENTAL ETHICS

Butane is one of the most dangerous substances you can work with for making hash because it is very explosive. Extract it in a well-ventilated area, such as a specially designed extraction room, or outside in an open area. Don't perform butane extractions indoors without adequate ventilation such as a lab hood.

Counter clockwise from bottom right: butane reservoir, Yellow Jacket pump, packed cylinder, viewing port, BHO collection reservoir.

Photo: David Downs

At room temperature butane is a flammable gas that's heavier than air. Instead of off-gassing and diffusing, butane pools on the floor and flows until it dissipates. If it comes in contact with an open flame, such as a pilot light or hot water heater, just a spark of static electricity, or a lit joint or lighter, it explodes.

Never smoke or use your cell phone around butane extraction equipment. Leave your lighter, smokes, and cell phone elsewhere so you don't absentmindedly try to use them. Do not wear synthetic fabric or wool. Static electricity starts more fires than smoking.

Butane has a lower explosion limit of 1.6% and an upper limit of 8.75%, meaning air becomes explosive when it is being mixed to only 1.6% butane. That's a very wide band of flammability.

In Colorado, butane extraction is subject to heavy regulation, and can only be performed in industrial zones. Manufacturers are required to operate special, flame-resistant rooms, with hydrocarbon meters hooked up to automatic ventilators. These facilities must pass official inspections before they can be used.

Although fire hazards are a real problem, butane is not responsible for environmental damage. Open-system extractors dump butane directly into the atmosphere, but it breaks apart naturally in a few days without causing environmental damage. Even so, *Beyond Buds* strongly endorses methods that recapture butane. The State of Colorado mandates that all BHO production be done on recapture systems. It is safer and more cost-effective than open-ended methods.

BUTANE EXTRACTS— THE CLOSED-LOOP METHOD

Introduction to Recapture Gear

All butane extraction systems contain some common elements, although there are many variations on the theme.

1. Butane reservoir—the butane tank holds the liquid butane, the solvent for the extraction

2. Trim tube—a stainless steel cylinder that is packed with trim

3. BHO vessel—the tank used to catch and hold the raw solution of butane and the extracted cannabinoids, waxes, etc.

4. Vacuum pump—a butane-proof, high-quality, high-speed pump used to create the vacuum or pressure needed to use the extractor

5. Vacuum oven—an industrial oven that pairs with a pump to create a vacuum inside, used to purge BHO of residual solvent

6. Fan—circulates air in open blasting environment to prevent potential build-up of explosive butane—only use fans that do not produce an open spark

A vacuum oven used to purge BHO.

Photo: David Downs

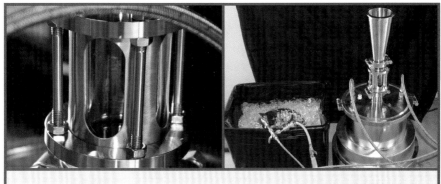

Professional equipment such as the Bhogart Extractor controls temperature and pressure. Works with a pump that increases the extraction speed and recovers solvents safely.

Photo: Bhogart

Equipment

- N-butane tanks

- Butane extractor with recapture (Bhogart 304 series stainless steel, tig-welded, 1-lb extractor)

- Filters (Whatman lab-grade, medium and slow filters)

- Source plant material (freshly dried and cured, trichome-rich, cleaned and chopped up)

- Oilless refrigeration recovery pump (Yellow Jacket)

- Vacuum oven (Across International vacuum drying oven, 0.9 cu ft)

- Multistage vacuum pump for oven (8 or higher CFM)

- Safety glasses

- Gas mask

- Cold-resistant lab gloves

- Implements: dishes, trays, scrapers, jars

- Laser thermometer

- Chemical fire extinguisher

- Fireproof suit

Obtaining Butane

Butane is a simple hydrocarbon molecule found in natural gas. It's one of a family of simple organic molecules that include ethane, methane, and propane. After it is pumped from natural gas wells, it is purified and compressed into liquid form for storage and use.

Use lab-grade, 99.5% pure or 99.9% pure butane, called instrument n-butane, from one of the major national suppliers. A tank the size of a small propane tank can be used to extract roughly 20 pounds of cannabis.

Avoid small cans of butane. No matter the alleged purity, consumer-grade cans of butane contain impurities, often introduced at the individual can level. Various oils are used as propelling agents, or to lubricate the machinery to fill the lighter fluid replacement cans, protect the can linings from rust, or prevent clogging. The mystery oil that is part of the production process does not have to be disclosed, and is listed in the ingredients as "one percent other." Extractors can be used to purify cheap butane and remove the mystery oil.

Preparation

Clean all parts with denatured alcohol.

Plant material should be fresh-cured and very dry. Store-bought cannabis averages 6% water by dry weight. Solvent hash plants needs to get under 1% water. Desiccants can be used to reduce the plant's water content, but the most reliable way of reducing moisture is to warm the cured herb in the oven at 120°F (49°C) for ten minutes. Either way, drying sacrifices terpenes that are volatile at low temperatures.

A packed cylinder should be firm and uniform but not too tight.

Photo: David Downs

Add one pound of chopped trim or buds to the trim tube on top of the chamber. Small, untrimmed, pea-sized nugs can be used. They make a fine grade of wax. Use a wooden dowel to pack it firm and uniform but not tight.

Blasting

Recapture extractors run in a big loop, with the ability of the operator to interrupt the circuit and send the solvent into a frozen recovery tank.

Install filters. Assemble collection vessel, viewing chamber, valves, packed trim tube, and shower head ball cap. Use the vacuum pump to pull the entire system down to a full vacuum (-20–30 mm Hg) in the system. This vacuum will help you find any leaks in the system before it is used. It also pulls any

BHO collection vessel being chilled.

Photo: David Downs

remaining water out of the system, and helps pull the butane out of its reservoir, through the plant matter, and into the catching bucket.

Check all connections. Make sure the clamps are really tight and the system is truly closed.

After the system is tested for leaks, warm up the butane reservoir with a hot water bath to give it some pressure, attach it to the system, and slowly open the butane tank valve. The liquid solvent will rush through the tubes, and begin filling up the trim tube. A manual butterfly valve sends the solution in the tube through the filters, past the viewing vessel, to pool in the collection reservoir.

At first, the system yields super high-end white, amber, or clear extract. The longer you run the system, the more cannabinoids are yielded, but the extract also becomes darker and lower quality from plant waxes and other oil solubles.

Depending on the pump, a one-pound extractor takes about a half hour to run a barbecue-sized tank of butane through three times. Check the pressure gauges regularly.

Purging/Achieving Different Consistencies/ Decarboxylating

Purging

The extraction process initially results in a solution of solvent and extract. Removing the solvent leads to the different consistencies in BHO. A proper purge can take days and a lot of patience.

Butane has a low boiling point, 31.5°F (-0.3°C). The collection reservoir gets very cold, around 32°F (0°C). The liquid butane takes en-

Closed-loop systems prevent you from seeing what's going on inside, save for the viewing vessel.

Mr. Nice B. Supermelt.

NYC Diesel Supermelt.

Photos: Nadim Sabella Photography

ergy from the environment as it converts back to gas. As the butane returns to a gas temperature in the collection tray, it is re-captured and either recirculated through the system or stored for future use.

There are two ways to prepare butane for storage: freezing or squeezing. The freezing recapture entails cooling the gas enough to store it as a liquid, while squeez-ing involves using pressure to return bu-tane to its liquid state for storage.

Use the vacuum pump on the extractor to perform the first purge. Extraction ma-chine makers often modify the collection chamber with a double wall to flow warm water (68°F [20°C] tops) around it to speed the recovery of the solvent. This is called a hot water bath and can be performed with open-ended systems as well.

Heat is the enemy of extraction. High temperature ruins shatter. Heat evaporates the terpenes that give great BHO its smell and flavors. Terpenes begin to evaporate at 68°F (20°C). Heat promotes hash decarboxylation, turning it into a dark oil suitable only for making edibles. Pay special attention to heat at all times. (See Decarbox-ylation section below for further information.)

After the initial purge, the ma-terial will no longer be a pool of liquid, or transparent, but rather more like a thick, goopy, runny toothpaste. You can take it out drier or wetter, depending on your goals of making shatter versus oil versus edibles.

Dump the goop onto a Pyrex dish, then scrape it onto parch-

This pre-purged BHO scraped from the vessel has great color and consistency.

Photo: David Downs

ment paper. Fold the parchment paper into little parchment trays with two- to three-inch walls. Preheat the oven to 94°F–98°F (34°C–37°C).

Now it's time to apply gentle heat under low pressure to finish purging and processing the batch. BHO is categorized by consistency, with shatter being the most prized. Next comes honeycomb, budder, wax, and oil.

The goal at all times should be the lightest color possible and an extremely dry quality. Great shatter is clear like amber glass, contains no bubbles, and breaks at room temperature. Honeycomb (wax) should be very pale, opaque, or translucent, dry and crumbly. Budder has more of a warm taffy quality to it, while oil is viscous yet tacky.

Shatter

Aim to make shatter. It's the hardest to make, requiring lower heat and a longer period of time in a vacuum oven.

For shatter, place the thick, goopy, pre-purged resin on parchment paper in a small oven rack, and place it in a vacuum oven at about 98°F (37°C) and at least -600 mm Hg (Torr) pressure for anywhere from 24 to 36 hours, interrupted by flushes of fresh air and slab-flipping. Temperatures and pressure can vary widely. Torr or mm Hg is a measure of pressure—which is the ratio of force to the area over which that force is distributed. Torr or mm Hg refers to milligrams of mercury, but a more common measure in America would be pounds per square inch, or psi. Pressure mea-

Extractions made with buds only, called "nug runs," yield very blond, super high-quality extracts.

Photo: David Downs

The Pure Sativa Supermelt.

Photo: Nadim Sabella Photography

BHO Honeycomb.

Photo: Steep Hill Halent

Kandy Jack Shatter.

Photo: David Downs

surement converters are available online and -600 mm Hg (Torr) equals -11.6 psi. Across International makes a high-quality, entry-level vacuum drying oven.

At this point, the amount of residual butane in the solution is low so the butane is too diluted to explode. Butane degrades normal vacuum pumps. Use one that is designed to tolerate the chemical.

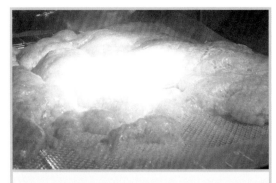

Pre-purged BHO loafs in a vac oven set to -30 mm Hg and 85°F (29°C).

Photo: David Downs

As the pressure drops and the temperature rises, the solvent boils out of the resin, causing the material to loaf up. If it boils violently, there is too much residual butane in it. Stop the process, take it out, and let it air dry or give it a hot bath to remove more butane. You don't want the slab loafing up more than a couple of inches. Increasing the air pressure reduces this loafing.

Heat also plays a crucial role by lowering the viscosity of the patty, allowing the butane to escape. Keep an eye on the bubbles. You're looking for large, thin, self-popping bubbles. If the bubble walls are thick and not popping, the patty is too viscous and needs a higher temperature to loosen up and allow the butane to purge. Conversely, if you are seeing no loaf expansion the heat may be too high.

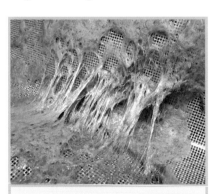

Note the viscosity of this lightly purged BHO after the second purge.

Photo: David Downs

Some go as low as 68°F (20°C) for strains that have the finished texture of sticky yet flexible tree sap. Some strains' finishing texture will be a tough sap that snaps if you pull it. They need heat of 85°F–100°F (29°C–38°C), versus 95°F–115°F (35°C–46°C) for strains that turn into good, solid shatter. Some strains' shatters require up to 125°F (52°C) for five to ten minutes for viscosity's sake, but anything over 115°F–120°F (46°C–49°C) causes most material to budder. (For more info, see Buddering below.) For a basic crumble wax, place the goopy BHO solution in a vac oven set to -600 mm Hg at 80°F–85°F (27°C–29°C) overnight.

Flush fresh air through the system every half hour and oven-vac for four or five hours until the slab looks settled.

Take the slab out and let it sit and settle for 20 or 30 minutes, but keep the oven on.

Place your slab-covered parchment paper on a cool surface, and pull the edge of the parchment paper down over the edge of the table. You want to see the shatter separate from the parchment

This finished shatter will crack or pull and snap at room temperature, is bone-dry, and is see-through with no impurities.

Photo: David Downs

paper. If it's sappy, lower the oven temp to 70°F (21°C) or 80°F (27°C) and give it four more hours in the vacuum oven. If it's stable, put on powderless silicone gloves, and flip the slab. Consolidate edge oil into the main body by folding it onto the top.

Flip the patty every 12 hours, because pockets of butane get trapped between the bottom of the patty and the parchment paper. Check to make sure the heat is transferring through the whole resin.

Repeat this gentle heat-and-pressure-purging process three or four times over a couple of days.

The low pressure and slight heat over a long period of time results in an amber-colored, transparent, crystalline, amorphous solid. It should be brittle, or at least pull and snap at room temperature.

You know you're done when you see very little slab activity in the vac oven, and it tests well below the 5,000 ppm threshold. Send a sample out to a lab to test it.

Buddering

If the shatter turns from clear to opaque, a process called buddering has occurred. The process is a one-way street. Once a shatter budders it must go through a complex process to get it back to true shatter. (See "Knottyy's BHO Budder to Shatter Tutorial" on YouTube.)

BHO of this consistency is called wax, budder, crumble, etc.

Photo: David Downs

BHO Shatter.

Photo: Steep Hill Halent

Many strains including Blue Dream and Grand Daddy Purple are notorious for auto-buddering—that is, the waxes in the solution hydrate and nucleate, or clump up. (OGs and Blue Dream tend to have a lot of wax in them.) Despite the most careful efforts to create shatter, the resin turns opaque during purging. At that point, it's best to make honeycomb.

Shatter turns to budder when heated too long, and even the finest shatter turns to budder eventually during storage. It's thought that the process of auto-buddering occurs when heavier fats and lipids precipitate out of the solution with the rest of the cannabinoid/terpene matrix. Buddering often starts in one corner of the resin patty, and spreads across the entire piece.

If buddering has occurred, you can heat the resin to a honeycomb consistency, whip it into budder, or heat it down to oil.

MIXING SOLVENTS

Mixing solvents slightly changes the mix's solubility, making it better suited to extracting specific terpenes in a particular strain.

Butane is a very simple organic molecule consisting of a chain of 4 carbon atoms with hydrogen atoms attached to them. Shortening or increasing the carbon chain yields propane (3 carbon atoms), and ethane (2), and methane (1), as well as pentane (5) and hexane (6). You can adjust the amount of n-butane in conjunction with its closest relatives—isobutane, propane, and pentane—to best suit the strain or desired consistency.

For example, n-butane has a slight water solubility. At 68°F (20°C), it is 0.0325% soluble, not 0%, so it's still soluble enough to pick up undesirable water solubles. One liter of n-butane can dissolve 32.5 ml of water. With water comes water solubles like chlorophyll and plant alkaloids, which taste bad. Pentane has zero water solubility.

Shatter.

: Steep Hill Halent

Lamb's Bread Shatter.

Photo: Nadim Sabella Photography

Mesozoic Amber Shatter.

Photo: Nadim Sabella Photography

BHO Shatter.

Photo: Steep Hill Halent

Leaving shatter in the vac oven at 120°F–130°F (49°C–54°C) for several hours results in a honeycomb-like wafer. More butane is removed when the temperature is raised and the pressure lowered, but it also removes more terpenes.

More heat and low pressure cause the honeycomb to melt back down to an overpurged, condensed plant oil.

BUTANE EXTRACTS— THE OPEN-ENDED METHOD

Equipment

- Butane canisters (one canister per ounce)

- Thick-gauge, 2"-wide, 25"-long Pyrex glass or stainless steel extraction tubes (stainless steel is stronger; Pyrex is easier to see what's going on inside the tube)

- Coffee filters (unbleached)

- Source plant material (trichome-rich, fresh-cured, cleaned of debris, chopped up)

- Large Pyrex casserole dishes for catching trays for solution

- Parchment paper

- Safety glasses

- Organic vapor-rated gas mask

- Large fan

- Hot plate

- Flame- and cold-resistant gloves

- Implements: dishes, trays, scrapers, jars

- Powderless latex gloves

- Laser thermometer

- Chemical fire extinguisher

- Fireproof suit

Obtaining Butane

Open-ended extraction is far less efficient (and hence, more expensive) than closed-loop. Since it doesn't reuse butane, it requires about 80 normal-sized canisters to extract from about five pounds of plant material (versus the equivalent of 32 canisters in closed-loop). If you cannot avoid cans of butane lighter fluid select a 5X or above quality fluid. There are many brands marketed for just this purpose. Stay away from Ronson and stove fuels—they contain poisonous additives. (See Tips/Reminders below.)

Preparation

Set up your extractor in a well-ventilated area during a cool, dry day.

Use very dry plant material. However, drying also sacrifices terpenes that are volatile at low temperatures.

Tightly affix filters to the bottom of the tube using hose clamps. Don't over-tighten, as you can crack Pyrex.

Add chopped trim and buds to the trim tube. Some people use small, un-trimmed, pea-sized nugs. Use a wooden dowel to pack it firm and uniform but not tight. An overpacked glass tube can shatter under pressure, or cause the bottom filter to pop off, blowing cannabis into the BHO.

Affix the canister discharge cap to the top of the tube. Alternatively, some open extraction tubes terminate in a hole that fits butane canisters, so you don't need a cap.

Set the tube up vertically with the filtered end at the bottom and the canister discharge cap end at the top.

Place a large Pyrex dish underneath the tube.

Position the fan so it blows fresh air at the extractor and worker, and pushes gas away from them.

Blasting

Discharge individual canisters into the hole in the egg-shaped top of the tube. Pressurized liquid butane will run through the material and eventually begin seeping through the filter and pooling in the Pyrex tray.

The tube will get cold during extraction and attract moisture from the air. This dew can freeze and break a glass tube. Stainless steel is a better choice. It's stronger and will not break.

The Pyrex tray of liquid solution will also get very cold. Take care to prevent dust or debris from blowing into the tray.

Mean Skreenz filters are made with chemical- and solvent-resistant material for use in the extraction of essential oils.

Photo: Ed Rosenthal

Purging/Achieving Different Consistencies/Decarboxylating

Purging

You can quickly and easily dewax the solution using dry ice. (See Winterizing below.)

If left outside in a well-ventilated area for a day to air purge, you'll be left with a waxy, yellow concentrate.

After dewaxing, speed up the purging process by using a hot plate set to 90°F–100°F (32°C–38°C) with a double boiler, in a well-ventilated area accompanied by a fan, to gently warm the solution. The BHO boils as the solvent quickly evaporates.

Be careful. This is the most dangerous stage of open-ended blasting. The vast majority of liquid butane evaporates into the atmosphere and travels along the ground looking for a spark to explode. Exercise maximum caution when double boiling. Also, you can use a breathable, water-resistant screen of some type over the Pyrex dish at this stage to keep dirt, dust, and debris from blowing into your solution from the fan.

It takes between 15 minutes to an hour to purge most of the butane out of the BHO using a hot plate and double boiler. The end material should have the consistency of maple syrup, and will be ready for the vacuum oven. If you leave it on the hot plate for too long it will get drier, and you'll end up with a mixture of budder and shatter in the tray.

A hot plate is also warm enough to burn off terpenes.

For a more thorough, professional purging, use a vacuum oven. (See Closed-Loop Method above.)

Variations

Purging

People use different combinations of temperature and pressure of the vacuum oven which affect the consistency.

A collection of dried waxes separated from their solution by winterization.

Photo: David Downs

This Buchner for an open-ended extraction consists of a broad funnel fitted with a stone filter and a flask underneath.

Photo: David Downs

Winterizing

Winterizing liquid solutions removes the wax content so the material develops a shatter consistency. Winterizing involves freezing the raw solution for 36 to 40 hours. The cold temperature causes the plant wax to precipitate and collect on the surface where it can be skimmed out. Winterizing shatter results in a much smoother smoke, because the heavy waxes are gone. Separated out, the wax can be used to make a candle.

You can winterize an open-loop system with dry ice or a Buchner—a glass beaker funnel fitted with a special 1.5-micron pumice stone that's super-chilled. For dry ice, place slabs of ice underneath the Pyrex dish used to catch the raw solution during extraction. The cold from the dry ice will cause the waxes and lipids to sink to the bottom of the Pyrex and congeal on it. Dump the remaining dewaxed solution into a clean Pyrex dish. For a Buchner, the raw solution is poured into the Buchner funnel and a hand pump is used to pull the BHO through the cold stone matrix, which holds on to the waxes while the rest of the solution falls through into the Erlenmeyer flask.

Some recapture units offer in-line winterization, which is a special stage in the process where the raw solution sits in a steel drum surrounded by a layer of dry ice. The dry ice chills the drum, and the waxes in the BHO collect on its sides.

Winterizing can be very dangerous. Do not simply stick a mason jar full of liquid butane solution in the freezer—you are making a bomb. The butane will evaporate out of the jar, flow down and out of the freezer until it finds a spark and explodes. Some professionals collect the raw solution in a stainless steel pressure pot, add in more liquid butane, and place it in an explosion-proof freezer that is specially well-ventilated. We repeat: **Placing butane in a freezer can result in a massive explosion.**

Decarboxylation

If the BHO is to be used in edibles, it needs to be decarboxylated because THCA's COOH carboxyl group makes it unable to pass the blood-brain barrier.

The COOH breaks apart from the THC over time, but you can speed up this process exponentially with heat.

THCA and CBDA decarboxylate into THC and CBD beginning at 222°F (106°C).

It's super easy to decarboxylate purged BHO—just double boil it in a water bath set to above 222°F (106°C). When the BHO gets warm enough it'll suddenly start producing CO_2 bubbles. Stir the BHO. When the bubbles suddenly start to taper off significantly, the BHO is mostly decarboxylated.

The wrinkle is, the same heat that turns THCA into THC also turns THC into cannabinol (CBN), which is more sedative than THC. When THCA is 70% decarboxylated into THC, the rate of THC-to-CBN production eclipses the rate of decarboxylation from THCA to THC.

So, when the bubble formation suddenly tapers off, the oil has reached the maximum head effect. Further heat makes it more sedative.

BHO that is going to be smoked or vaped does not need to be decarboxylated. The lighter or nail will take care of that instantly.

Tips/Reminders

- Water is the enemy of solvent extraction. Water is the most universal of solvents and it is very polar. It has spare electrons that interact with anything that is polar. Trichomes are nonpolar due to their waxy, oily covering. THCA is slightly polar, and bound up in the wax. Water in the butane extractor or plant material raises the polarity of the system, decreasing the solubility of the solvent and preventing butane from doing its job. Keep water out of the extraction system, and run the process in a room with very low humidity.

- High heat is an enemy. Even low heat can make the delicate flavors and smells of cannabis disappear, and very high temperatures degrade THC. Dissolved hash will also darken, leading to a far less desirable end result. Work in a cool, dry room, and do not overheat during purging. Terpenes begin to burn off at 68°F (20°C).

- Test the vacuum oven by pulling it down to the lowest it will go and waiting an hour. If the vacuum is lost it means there is a leak.

- Make sure the air pressure gauges on the vacuum oven are in good working order.

- If you pull a vacuum too fast on a resin that is too liquid the violent boiling can make a mess. Bring the pressure down slowly to keep the resin calm.

- Raise the temperature slowly on the vacuum oven or you can easily overshoot it and burn the resin.

- Be careful with extreme vacuum pressure. A super-strong vacuum pump is not needed. At 99.999% vacuum (.01 Torr), THC boils at 23°F (-5°C). Don't go below a 99.2% vacuum or 1.5 Torr (1500 microns).

- Cannabis is just like any other produce; it browns as it ages. That includes the trichomes or any extract made from it. Fresher is always better.

- For best taste, fresh, dried material is ideal. Older material will just taste like hash. The degree of drying and curing is critical to maintain maximum flavor and taste. BHO from buds is called a "nug run" and tastes better than trim.

- If you can't get instrument-grade n-butane, use butane advertised in appropriate magazines and in appropriate stores, but do some homework. Check out the MSDS (material safety data sheet) from the specific manufacturer, showing the product's contents on the Internet. Avoid anything with mercap or Butadiene. Ingredients that comprise less than 1% of the fluid do not appear on material safety data sheets. If the MSDS looks all right, spray a five-second burst on a mirror or clean glass pane and let it completely evaporate. Check for residue. Smell it for mercaps—you can't miss them.

- Consumer brands Colibri, King, Lucienne, Newport, and Vector—4X or higher—work well. The X refers to how pure the product is in terms of how much paraffin wax has been taken out of the gas.

- Do not use Poly Vinyl Chloride (PVC), Acrylonitrile Butadiene Styrene (ABS), or Low Density Poly Ethylene (LDPE) in your extraction equipment, as the butane leaches chemicals out of the plastic, and they will end up in the hash. Stainless steel is best. Borosilicate glass may break in cold, wet weather.

- Watch your ambient humidity. Butane boils at room temperature, pulling heat from the air, and getting very cold, causing condensation of ambient humidity. This adds water to your solution and water is the enemy.

- Use filters carefully. They are a critical bottleneck in both open and closed-loop extraction. Clean reusable filters every time before a new run. Don't use too many disposable filters. Both dirty reusable filters

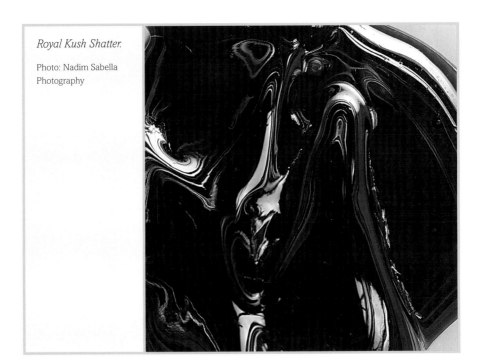

Royal Kush Shatter.

Photo: Nadim Sabella
Photography

and too many disposable filters can clog up your system, and significantly delay or even ruin the extraction process.

- Cleanliness and orderliness are mandatory in extraction. Look around your room right now. Make sure the workspace is orderly and clean. Make sure all the tools you might need are in place.

- Be prepared to encounter setbacks, especially in pursuit of excellence. Slightly tweaking a process or trying a new one may create problems. Even dialed-in systems go haywire from equipment malfunction. Murphy's Law applies.

Curing/Pressing/Storage

Cure fresh shatter in a cool, dry room at 40°F–60°F (4°C–16°C) with under 30% humidity for at least a day. The curing process can lock in the shatter and prevent auto-buddering during storage.

BHO does not need to be pressed and is best stored on parchment paper in a sealed glass jar in a cool, dark place where it will not be exposed to humidity.

Due to their nonstick surface, silicone containers are often used for storage of BHO.

Headband CO$_2$ Shatter.

Photo: Nadim Sabella Photography

Chapter 8.

CO$_2$ Extracts—

Making Concentrates

Marijuana extraction technology is leapfrogging into the future. That future is largely considered to belong to carbon dioxide, which normally exists as 0.039% of the air in our atmosphere.

We all have a basic understanding of CO$_2$. Plants use it. Humans exhale it. At atmospheric pressure, CO$_2$ has no liquid state. It goes from a solid (dry ice) directly to a gas. But at pressures greater than 5.1 standard atmospheres, it does liquefy.

Extract artists exploit the physical properties of liquid and "supercritical" CO$_2$ to extract and concentrate cannabinoids found on marijuana plants. The machines are expensive and require several days of training to learn how to operate, but have a number of advantages. They are far safer to operate than butane extractors, because carbon dioxide is not flammable. And any CO$_2$ left in an extract is harmless, whereas a large amount of residual butane in poorly purged BHO is not healthy.

Large extraction companies are turning to CO$_2$ because the equipment converts large amounts of leaf and trim into some of the cleanest, most valuable cannabis products in the world.

CO_2 extracts are four to five times as concentrated as the best buds yet they can be inhaled without the irritation of smoking raw cannabis. CO_2 extracts can also be used to make super-potent edibles, topicals, and other marijuana-infused products.

OVERVIEW

CO_2 extraction involves using cool, pressurized carbon dioxide in either liquid or supercritical form to strip the psychoactive ingredients from the surface of the cannabis plant. The CO_2 is then purged from the solution, leaving the plant's waxes, fats, lipids, and cannabinoids behind. The process requires tanks of CO_2 and an extractor designed to function under the extreme cold and pressure of the process.

Gas is liquefied then pumped through a pressure vessel packed with cannabis. The resulting mix is depressurized in a separator vessel, resulting in the cannabinoids, oils, waxes, and anything else in the solution falling out of the mix as the CO_2 exits the vessel and is vented off.

"Supercritical" CO_2 extraction refers to extractions that occur beyond the "critical point" of carbon dioxide. Normally we think of CO_2 in gas, liquid, or solid form. But past CO_2's critical point, the molecule ceases to exist as a typical solid, liquid, or gas. Supercritical CO_2 looks like a very dense fog.

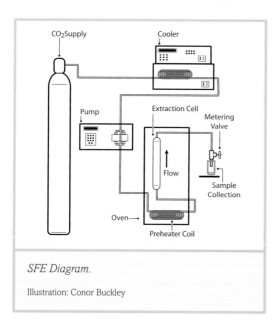

SFE Diagram.

Illustration: Conor Buckley

Supercritical fluid has no surface tension. It moves through the vegetative material like a gas and dissolves trichomes.

Carbon dioxide's supercritical state results from a combination of temperature and pressure. CO_2's supercritical range begins at 87°F (30°C) and 1070 psi. (By contrast, water goes supercritical at 700°F [371°C] and 4000 psi.) Supercritical fluid extraction (SFE) is usually performed at 5000 to 8000 psi.

"Subcritical" CO_2 extraction uses CO_2 in its liquid state, below its critical point. Pressure of between 800 and 1500 psi is applied to CO_2 at a temperature of 35°F (2°C)–55°F (13°C). The CO_2 liquid is pumped through plant material and it dissolves the oils and terpenes. Then the CO_2 is decompressed and returns to its gaseous state. The oils, consisting mostly of cannabinoids, terpenes, and waxes, precipitate out and are collected on a nearby surface.

Supercritical fluid extraction has some advantages over subcritical (liquid) extraction. Supercritical fluids are faster extractors because of their low viscosities and high diffusiveness. CO_2 is pumped through the extracting material 3 to 10 times using supercritical, rather than 10 to 40 times using subcritical. Another advantage is that it can be used to select particular molecules for extraction by manipulating pressure and temperature.

The downside is supercritical fluid CO_2 reacts with moisture to form carbonic acid, which turns oils rancid. For this reason all material used for extractions must be completely dry.

Supercritical CO_2 extraction is likely the future of legal, marijuana-infused products because manufacturers can pinpoint molecules they want to extract and leave everything else behind. The end product contains virtually no residual CO_2, which we inhale with every breath and which is harmless.

While CO_2 extractions create no harmful residues, BHO extractions do contain remnants of the extraction solvent, which makes many people reluctant to use these concentrates. Butane extraction has higher yields than CO_2, but butane is explosive, while CO_2 is not. CO_2 has much higher start-up costs than BHO as far as equipment. However, the start-up costs of a fully permitted, legal BHO extraction center can equal or surpass that of CO_2 extraction.

A CO_2 EXTRACTION METHOD

Equipment

This Hi-Flo system from Eden Labs can be used with a 5hp compressor for energy efficiency. The air-drive liquid CO_2 pump needs little maintenance.

Photo: Brad Huskinson

- Plant material (fresh, cured, very dry, and trichome rich, cleaned of all debris)

- Liquid CO_2 cylinder with dip tube (a 50-pound cylinder goes for about $20; you'll need 75 pounds to extract 5 liters)

- CO_2 extractor (Eden Labs 5 liter, 2000 psi; Waters SFE 500 (Super Fluid Extractor); Apeks 1500-1L)

TERMS OF EXTRACTION

Carbon dioxide extraction of cannabis fits into a broader practice of plant extraction that dates back hundreds of years. Plant extracts are used extensively in medicine and the perfume industry. The industry breaks plant extracts down in three general categories, each more refined: essential oils, concretes, and absolutes.

Essential Oils: An essential oil is a concentrated hydrophobic liquid containing the volatile aroma compounds and other "essential" molecules of a plant—including its lipids and, in the case of pot, its cannabinoids. Essential oils are obtained by pressure or steam, water, or dry distillation.

Concretes: Essential oil extracts made from hydrophobic solvent are called concretes and are a mixture of oil, waxes, resins, and other oil-soluble plant material, like THC. They can be hard, malleable, or viscous depending on wax content.

Absolutes: Concretes treated with another solvent to remove their waxes and leave just the fragrant, essential oil are called absolutes. They're usually highly concentrated viscous liquids but can be solid or semisolid.

- Industrial CO_2 pumps, rated anywhere from 5–10000 psi, .01–50 ml/min flow rate, +/-2% pressure accuracy; stainless steel fluid path

- Heater

- Chillers

- Condensing coil

- Cold gloves

- Pyrex dishes

Pre 97 Bubba CO_2 Oil by CO_2 Made requires little additional processing beyond the extraction process. CO_2 concentrates are made without heavy metals, hydrocarbon materials, or residual contaminants.

Introduction to Gear

Here are the basic components of a CO_2 supercritical extractor (SFE machine) from beginning to end:

- CO_2 supply—your tanks of CO_2

- Cooling bath/heat exchanger—to ensure CO_2 is in liquid state when it goes to pump

- CO_2 pump—the heart of the system; receives liquid CO_2 at 750 psi and takes it to supercritical levels

- Heater/heat exchanger—used to raise pressurized CO_2 to supercritical temperatures

- Extraction vessel—where CO_2 and plant matter meet and extraction occurs

- Back-pressure regulator—reduces pressure, turning supercritical CO_2 back to a gas, causing precipitation of solutes

- Fraction collector/collection vessel—where precipitated solutes collect

- Vent—where CO_2 comes out of the system

- CO_2 condenser/chiller—used to reliquefy CO_2 for recycling

System Setup and Checks

These units range in size from desktop to garage-sized and need to be placed in a structure that has enough power and ventilation, ideally something like a mechanic's bay. Smaller systems run on 110V, but larger systems usually use 220V circuits. The pumps, heat exchangers, and other equipment generate heat and noise, so the space must be able to accommodate it.

Each equipment manufacturer's machines have their own procedures and techniques. For that reason, the equipment comes with comprehensive guides. Some manufacturers provide personal training, since the process can be quite complex.

Key Tips

- Make sure the seals are tight, but don't overtighten or cross-thread them.

- Use a procedures guide, a safety checklist, and the same extraction process every time.

- Do not guess about procedures because it can be very dangerous.

Blasting

After your system is all set up and you are trained on it, follow the basic extraction steps below.

1. Warm everything up: Start up the chiller and the heat exchangers. They need a bit of time to warm water or cool coolant to their set points. Bringing hundreds of pounds of stainless steel extraction equipment to its specific operating temperatures can take 3–4 hours.

2. Load the extraction vessel with your prepared material and bolt the lid.

3. Pressure test the system for 15–20 minutes to make sure there are no leaks. Keep a watchful eye on the gauges looking for sudden pressure drops or temperature changes.

4. Extract: Send liquid CO_2 through the pump, which raises its pressure to 5000–8000 psi. The 80°F (27°C) heater makes the liquid go supercritical. The CO_2 mixes with the trim in the extraction vessel, dissolves the plant's oils, and flows out to the back-pressure regulator.

5. Precipitate: The back-pressure regulator takes the supercritical CO_2 solution from 5000+ psi to 45 psi, flashing it back to a gas and causing the essential oil to fall out.

6. Vent/Recirculate: CO_2 is then vented outside the building or sent to the compressor/chiller that reliquefies the CO_2 and sends it back to the beginning of the system. It can take 20 minutes to an hour to fully extract from trim, depending on vessel size.

7. Depressurize the extraction vessel and open the drain valve to receive the oil.

8. Clean: Run the system dry to clean it. Clean in between different strains and at the end of the day.

Tips

You'll get more consistent results at the low end of the supercritical range. The higher you go in the supercritical range, the hotter and more soluble the CO_2 becomes, which can burn cannabinoids, and extract plant matter.

As gas drains from the CO_2 tank, it depressurizes and cools. This can create bubbles or voids in the line, which can cause flow problems. Prevent these bubbles by not using nearly empty CO_2 tanks. Use a scale to keep an eye on how much CO_2 is left in a tank. When it gets to a certain weight indicating it is low, swap it out.

Keep the temperature in the extraction room at a consistent 65°F (18°C) and keep humidity as low as possible. Don't extract in hot environments; the ambient heat will work its way into your system and sap your yield.

Purchase an American-made extractor. You're going to need the manufacturer's staff to train you, and you're going to be calling them when you run into problems. An SFE machine is a very hands-on product.

The pump is the heart of the SFE system, and must be designed to withstand operating pressures and temperatures for prolonged periods of time. Waters, Apeks, and Eden Labs sell appropriate pumps. The pump is the part of the system that is most likely to require servicing, and they can run tens of thousands of dollars. Broken pumps are the chief cause of downtime. Prevent this by having a backup or replacement pump so the system can continue functioning while the pump is being serviced.

You can reuse your CO_2 a couple times. A compressor and

CO_2 RESOURCES

Apeks
ApeksSupercritical.com

Eden Labs
EdenLabs.com

Waters Corporation
Waters.com

chiller reliquefies CO_2, and charcoal microfilters scrub out the water and other impurities. Still it will eventually have to be vented off. It is still suitable to use for enriching gardens with CO_2.

Purging

With CO_2 you don't really have to purge unless you are using a high amount of cosolvent. (Cosolvents, often ethyl alcohol, are used in some machines.)

Raw CO_2 oil comes out of the drain valve bright red, yellow, orange, or amber. If it's green, chlorophyll has been extracted. Most likely one of five things is happening: the pressure is too high; the temperature is too high; the trim is old, stale, or wet. Moisture changes the pH of CO_2, making it more acidic and polar. Acidic, polar solvents extract chlorophyll and other undesired elements.

If used in an open system, the CO_2 evaporates to a gas from its supercritical or liquid state and returns to the atmosphere. Vent it outside or it can kill you. The process yields a thick oil. Strain and processing can play a role in determining how much wax is in the raw oil.

When the paste is left sitting in the open air it slowly settles into a blob, sort of like a bead of water on a hydrophobic surface, or into an oil-like consistency.

You can further alter this product for use in vape pens or edibles. Commercial manufacturers sometimes add propylene glycol to the oil to make it runnier for flowing into pens and cartridges. However, we don't recommend that you ingest one of the main ingredients of windshield washer fluid. By changing the techniques you can make different consistencies, such as a honeycomb-like crumble consistency, or slow-flowing or hardened oils by dewaxing the material (see below).

The Coldfinger from Eden Labs enables distillation at low temperatures and creates faster extraction.

Photo: Eden Labs

Winterization/Dewaxing

Winterization in chemistry refers to the removal of waxes from a solution, usually by means of cold temperature. There are several ways to dewax CO_2 oil in the depressurization stage of extraction. One way is to treat CO_2 oil with another solvent, usually alcohol, to dewax it. Winterization boosts THC levels from 50%–70% to 80%–90%, but the increase comes at the expense of terpenes, which are lost in the process.

Decarboxylation

In order to use CO_2 concentrates in edibles, they must first be decarboxylated. Decarboxylation is a process that uses heat to change raw THCA, CBDA, and other cannabinoid acids to their psychoactive, nonacid form. Decarboxylating a CO_2 extract requires taking it up to 220°F (104°C)–240°F (115°C) for a certain period of time depending on the amount of oil you have. Even though CBD is nonpsychoactive, you still need to use heat to remove the acid from the CBD or your body cannot use it as it would if smoked.

Variations

Strain, growing environment, harvest time, curing method and length, and batch size all play roles in varied outcomes of CO_2 extraction.

One strain may extract twice as fast as another strain. Strains vary in their yield, color of the oil, and consistency. Cannabinoid ratios play a role in solubility, color, taste, and smell.

Using all buds, small nugs, trim, or a combination thereof also results in different quality oils.

Keep variables to a minimum to get a repeatable outcome. Fully automated computerized systems like an Apeks or Waters CO_2 SFE machine drastically reduce variability and produce more consistent oil compared to manual systems.

Storage/Pressing

Store CO_2 extracts in a cool, dark place in a silicone container, which concentrates don't stick to. Parchment paper can also be used because concentrates don't adhere to it. They do stick to Pyrex and stainless steel.

Long-term exposure to air or light causes unwanted reactions with the active ingredients.

CO_2 oil or honeycomb—the two most common consistencies—do not need pressing. The trichome heads were already broken in the violent extraction process and the active compounds dissolved into the solution before being chilled out of it.

People are using CO_2 oil in vape pens, oil rigs, heath stones, or over a bowl of flowers. The flowers act as a sponge and prevent the heated CO_2 extract—which liquefies—from running through a pipe.

Eden Labs

Company Spotlight

Eden Labs founder Fritz Chess created the company in 1996 to reinvent standard scientific extraction equipment. The first was the Coldfinger Home Unit, an updated version of the standard Sohxlet extractor used in labs since 1921. The Coldfinger method takes advantage of the evaporation and condensation principle that creates rainfall. A perforated basket of herb is suspended between a cooled condenser and a heated pool of solvent. The heat causes solvent evaporation, which then liquefies on the cooler condenser and saturates the herb with solvent, resulting in a steady drip of extract into the bottom of the flask.

In 1997, Eden Labs created a CO_2 extractor based on the Coldfinger design, but it remained slow and required maintenance. In 2012, they started research and development for the Hi-Flo, a unique supercritical CO_2 system. After a year's worth of R&D, the Eden Labs team redesigned the pumping system, the solvent recovery system, and the vessel closures to create a more efficient CO_2 design.

In the Hi-Flo process, liquid CO_2 is pumped through a pressure vessel filled with dried, ground herb. The CO_2 dissolves plant oils and carries them to a separator where the stream is depressurized and heated, causing the CO_2 to flash vaporize and drop the oil to the bottom of the separator. The CO_2 drops into an accumulator and flows back to the pump and extractor vessel in a continuous loop. At the end of the cycle, the CO_2 is pumped back to a storage vessel so the separator can be opened to collect the extract.

The Commercial Vacuum Distiller offers five methods of extraction and four methods of distillation, and has multiple upgrades allowing for use with a variety of gases and solvents, as well as the ability to act as a fractionating separator. It can be fully automated.

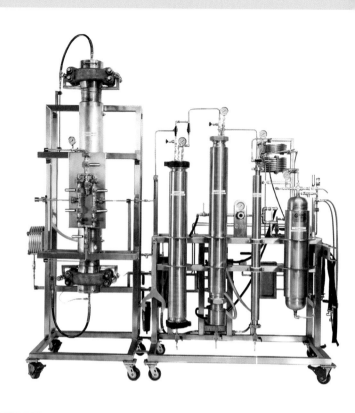
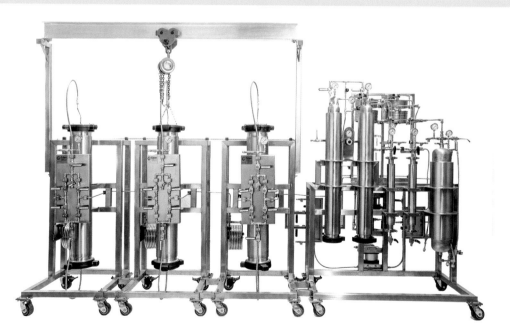

Alcohol- and glycerin-based tinctures.

Photo: Steep Hill Halent

Chapter 9.

Tinctures—

Alcohol and Glycerin

Before cannabis prohibition tinctures were the most common way of buying and consuming marijuana in America. Recently, they've been making a comeback. Commercially prepared tinctures are now available in dispensaries in many states. Tinctures are discreet to use and are quite easy to make at home.

A tincture is a concentrated extract of any herb in liquid—usually alcohol, sometimes glycerin—that is taken by mouth as a drop on or under the tongue. Alcohol is used to separate the cannabinoids, terpenes, and other essential oils from the marijuana plant material and acts as a preservative. In herbal medicine, tinctures are commonly 25% alcohol, which is achieved by diluting the mixture with water. People who do not want to consume alcohol may opt for glycerin-based tinctures.

Methods of making alcohol tinctures of marijuana vary from extremely simple and low tech to complex distillation apparatuses that produce highly purified cannabis oil. The easiest way to make tinctures is an alcohol soak. All that's required is a bottle of 100 proof or higher drinking alcohol and cannabis leaf, trim, bud, or kief. Add the cannabis to the liquor, let it soak for at least a week, then strain (or not) and enjoy.

CHOOSING THE ALCOHOL

No matter what type of marijuana is going into the tincture, starting with a quality solvent is important. The purist grade alcohol is USP medical-grade 190- or 200-proof neutral grain spirits. It is available from laboratory supply companies.

More commonly available is 190-proof Everclear brand alcohol, which can be found at liquor stores in 40 of the 50 states. Note that Everclear is marketed in two strengths: 150 proof (75% alcohol) and 190 proof (95% alcohol). Get the 190. Sale of Everclear 190 is banned in California, Florida, Hawaii, Iowa, Maine, Minnesota, New York, Nevada, Ohio, and Washington.

An alternative high-proof option that is available in some of those states and online is an extremely pure form of Polish vodka called Spirytus that comes in at 192 proof, or a percent purer than Everclear. Polmos Spirytus, Spirytus Rektyfikowany, and Baks Spirytus are some of the brands that can be found in the United States.

If these purified options are unavailable or you are interested in a little flavor, other high-proof liquors can be used, such as Bacardi 151-proof rum. There are a number of brands of 100–120-proof vodkas and rums that can be used.

TYPES OF ALCOHOL

Know the difference between ethanol alcohol versus denatured and isopropyl alcohol. Ethanol-based tinctures and extracts can be ingested or used topically. Extracts made with isopropyl alcohol are poisonous and cannot be ingested safely. They can only be used externally.

Ethanol is sometimes called ethyl alcohol. If buying medical- or laboratory-grade ethanol, double check to be sure that it has not been denatured. Denatured ethanol is the kind put in vehicles.

Denatured ethanol and isopropyl are poisonous taken internally and can kill you. They can be used to make topical products for external use only. They should never be consumed or ingested.

THE HERB

Tinctures made with different varieties of marijuana have varying effects because of the entourage effects that the terpenes, the odor molecules, create. Plant parts being used, maturity at harvest, and post-harvest processing all play a part in determining the tincture's potency. Leaf, trim, bud, kief, and hash are some of the choices, and all are used.

Commercially available Full Extract Cannabis Oil is refined using only food-grade ethyl alcohol and can be used topically and internally.

Photo: Nadim Sabella Photography

When used for medicinal purposes, a tincture with CBD as well as THC may be beneficial. Some medical tincture makers have adopted cold-processing methods to avoid decarboxylating the cannabinoid acids. Not converting THCA to THC increases possible dosage levels because the THCA does not activate the high, but its medical qualities remain.

If marijuana has been dried and cured as it would be for smoking, some decarboxylation will have already taken place, so THC and CBD will be present without using heat, just not as much. Raw fresh or dried marijuana leaves can be used to make tinctures, though the resulting product may have a chlorophyll flavor. Gently soaking the dried marijuana in water removes some of the chlorophyll, which dissolves in water. Adding a bit of honey to the finished tincture can make it more palatable.

If using fresh plant material, fill a glass container with herb, then add alcohol (ethanol) to the top. If using powdered, dried herb, figure roughly one ounce of weed for every four ounces of alcohol. Use a butter knife to stir the mixture to release air bubbles trapped in the plant material. Cover it. Let it steep in a cool, dark space for two weeks or more. Shake the container daily to mix the ingredients and help the alcohol dissolve the terpenes and cannabinoids. Then strain out the plant material using a sieve lined with cheesecloth set on a glass or metal bowl. The length of time it steeps results in slightly different tinctures. A longer soak extracts more cannabinoids and essential oils, making it stronger and more concentrated, but it also leaches out more of the plant's other chemicals, such as chlorophyll. Splitting a batch between several jars that can be left to steep for differing amounts of time can help you determine what works best for you.

If you're using dried marijuana and want a tincture with the most punch possible, carefully heat the marijuana first. Just spread the leaves, trim, or bud on a cookie sheet and put it in the oven at 125°F (52°C) for an hour. This decarboxylates the THCA and other cannabinoid acids to a more potent form. Heating at a higher temperature would cause most of the terpenes, the odor molecules, to evaporate. Higher temperatures also convert THC to the less

> **THE HISTORY OF HEMP TINCTURES**
>
> Tinctures were the delivery method Western medicine used for marijuana for more than 90 years. Major U.S. pharmaceutical companies produced them from the mid-nineteenth century until cannabis was removed from the United States Pharmacopeia in 1942. The Marihuana Tax Act of 1937 made production of cannabis medicines prohibitively expensive, and there was a turn away from botanical medicines to synthesized and purified drugs than could be injected. THC had not been discovered, and no one knew what was creating marijuana's effects or how to standardize them. This created significant quality control issues.
>
> Our ability to test for the cannabinoids provides the opportunity to produce dose-controlled medicines. GW Pharmaceuticals in the U.K. has registered Sativex, a 50:50 THC:CBD extract, and Epidiolex, a high-CBD extract. Both drugs are alcohol-based marijuana tinctures that are sprayed under the tongue. Dispensaries in some states sell many versions of tinctures, so patients have many choices.

potent, more sedative CBN. There is no need to grind the marijuana before adding it to alcohol because the cannabinoids and terpenes are almost all on the surface. Grinding results in more sludge collecting at the bottom.

When the same material is used repeatedly to extract cold-water hash, each pull will have a lower quality, with more vegetative material and a strong botanical smell, but it is excellent for making tinctures. Be sure to filter the collected material using screens, high-grade cheesecloth, or a coffee filter.

STRAINING

To strain the tincture, line a sieve or metal colander with cheesecloth and place it over a clean metal or glass bowl. Pick the type of cheesecloth based on how big the plant particles are that you want to catch. Cheesecloth comes in different grades, based on how tight the weave is, just as printing screens that can be used for sifting kief are graded based on how fine the mesh is. Cheesecloth grades range from the very loosely woven #10 to the extra-fine #90. Unlike the symmetrical mesh of metal and plastic sifting screens, the number of threads per inch in cheesecloth varies horizontally and vertically, as seen below.

Use a looser grade for straining freshly chopped plant material; it catches the plant material and does not clog. Cheesecloth grade #60 to grade #90 is best for straining ground and powdered dried herb for tincture making to avoid sludge build-up. Using fine-grade cloth requires patience because it takes a long time for the extract to seep through. Once gravity has done all it can to pull the tincture through, lift the cheese-cloth carefully up by the corners from the sieve and squeeze any remaining solution into the bowl.

If kief or powdered, dry herb is used to make tincture, even the finest cheesecloth or pastry cloth will let some sludge particles through. A second pass through a paper coffee filter or a #1 laboratory filter yields a cleaner, particulate-free product.

Another way to separate the

Grade	Vertical x Horizontal Threads per Inch
#10	20 x 12
#40	24 x 20
#50	28 x 24
#60	32 x 28
#90	44 x 36

dissolved THC and terpenes from the brew is to use a colander lined with cheesecloth to remove most of the particles. Squeeze the solution from the cloth. Place the cloth back in a bowl and add virgin alcohol. Dip the bag as if it were a teabag to capture more cannabinoids in the alcohol. Warming it gently on a well-ventilated electric stove to about 100°F (38°C) makes the cannabinoids more soluble. Careful: Alcohol fumes are explosive so this should be done in a well-ventilated space or outdoors. Add the new cannabinoid solution to the first one.

Place the solution in a wide-mouth glass jar or pitcher and cover it. Then let it sit in a cool dark place undisturbed for several days or more. Vegetative material mixed into the liquid will separate, either floating to the top or sinking to the bottom. The alcohol solution is fairly pure. Gently skim the floating material from the top. Then siphon the solution from the top, leaving the sunken particulates undisturbed. The siphoned solution can easily be purified further using fine filters, which it passes through very quickly.

ASK ED'S FAST-TRACK TINCTURE

Traditional tincture recipes talk about an aging process: "Let the mixture sit for…" The reason that the tincture gets stronger as it ages is that, at least in theory, more of the THC and other cannabinoids dissolve in the alcohol as time passes. This method speeds up the process by giving the dissolving cannabinoids a quick mechanical assist.

Equipment

- Disposable neoprene or latex gloves

- Blender

- Metal slotted serving spoon

- Colander

- Fine mesh strainer

- Glass or stainless steel bowl, sized to hold colander

- Cloth kitchen towel

- Amber or cobalt blue glass jar with sealing lid

- Funnel (optional)

Ingredients

- Bud, trim, or leaf material

- Grain neutral spirits such as Everclear or overproof alcohol such as 151 rum or vodka

Method

Weigh the marijuana. For every ounce of herb use ten fluid ounces of alcohol. A 750 ml bottle of alcohol is 25.4 fluid ounces, so a full bottle is good for just over two and a half ounces of weed.

Place the marijuana in a colander up to one-third full. Do not break up the leaves or buds so that the glands remain on the leaf surfaces. Place the marijuana-filled colander in a mixing bowl. Add enough cool—not cold—water so that the marijuana can spread out. Let the weed sit in the water bath for an hour or so to dissolve the nonactive, water-soluble pigments and carbohydrates from the plant material.

Pull the colander from the water and let the water strain out of the plant material. Wearing gloves, roll the marijuana into a ball. Wrap it in a clean dish towel and squeeze out as much water as possible.

Place the strained plant material in a blender. Add ten ounces of alcohol for each ounce of marijuana. Place the cover on the blender. Blend at the lowest setting for five minutes. Let it sit for an hour, and then blend on low again for five minutes. Pour the blend into a bowl or wide mouth pitcher. Let the mixture sit for a couple of hours so that the leaf floats to the top of the alcohol.

Using a slotted spoon, remove the large floating debris and put it in the fine mesh strainer with the mixing bowl underneath to catch the drainage. Using gloves, press the herb against the strainer to squeeze out the liquid into the bowl. Break up the ball and let it soak in a small amount of virgin alcohol to dissolve remaining cannabinoids. Then repeat the squeezing process, and discard the plant material. It can also be used as a poultice.

Pour the liquid through the fine mesh strainer over the bowl. Depending on how fine the mesh and how good the blender, you may see tiny insoluble plant particles in the bowl. If so, filter the tincture through a coffee filter or ultra-fine cheesecloth. If you are using a funnel for transferring the tincture to jars for storage, put the coffee filter or fine cheesecloth inside the funnel and filter while you fill. The tincture is ready to use but a little raw.

Test the tincture. Ideally a dose will be no less than a dropper full. If it is too strong, add alcohol or water. If it is not strong enough, concentrate it by evaporating some of the alcohol. Placing the marijuana in an open mixing bowl in a warm room speeds alcohol evaporation. Covering the bowl or jar with cheesecloth slows evaporation but keeps out dust and dander. Within a few hours the bowl will contain visibly less liquid. Once the tincture is concentrated

QUICK WASH METHOD

For the purest extract, a quick alcohol wash can be used. This method leaves more of the chlorophyll and other water-based chemicals behind and reduces the time the extracted oils are exposed to alcohol and any potential chemical changes.

- Start with dried, cured herb. Do not grind.

- Place on a cookie sheet in a 100°F (38°C) oven until bone-dry and brittle.

- Place the herb in a glass jar and put it in a freezer to dry further.

- Add high-proof ethyl alcohol and shake to make sure all the vegetation is thoroughly wet.

- Return jar to freezer for one minute.

- Remove jar from freezer, shake, and return to freezer for another minute.

- Repeat.

- After three minutes, remove jar and strain the mixture through a fine wire mesh that lets it drain quickly.

- Refilter using a coffee filter or a #1 laboratory filter.

- The resulting tincture can be used as is or reduced to oil.

- Reprocess the strained plant material for a second batch with different properties. Because the quick wash technique is so rapid, there will still be a considerable amount of cannabinoids remaining. If using kief or hash instead of trim or bud, you can skip the oven drying step.

to the strength desired, put it in a clean, dark glass container and seal it tightly. Store refrigerated in the dark. Long exposure to warmth and oxygen degrades cannabinoid content.

BOTTLING AND STORAGE

Once you've filtered the tincture, use a funnel to fill the storage bottles. Tincture bottles, sometimes called "Boston rounds," should be glass and either amber (brown) or cobalt blue. Do not use clear glass—light causes the cannabinoids to degrade. Do not use plastic bottles—the alcohol will leach potentially harmful chemicals from the plastic. Amber glass bottles are widely available in sizes from 0.5 ounces to 32 ounces. The most common sizes for use with droppers are between 0.5 and 4 ounces.

For applying the tincture, you will want at least one or two tops with built-in droppers sized to the depth of the bottle. For storage, use regular, solid screw caps; they seal better.

Label the tinctures by variety, solute, and date. Keep tinctures in a refrigerator, which slows degradation of cannabinoids to a crawl. They can be stored for years, without losing much potency.

REDUCING TINCTURES TO OIL

Cannabinoid-rich oil can easily be extracted from alcohol tinctures because alcohol evaporates rapidly, particularly when heat is applied.

A Slow but Safe No-Effort Method

Alcohol evaporates at room temperature, so leaving the top off the tincture bottle or putting the tincture in a bowl or pan for a while reduces it. This works, but it is slower. Remember to cover the jar, bowl, or pan with fine-grade cheesecloth to keep out dust and dander.

The Faster Heat Method

Alcohol boils at 173°F (78°C), below the temperature at which cannabinoids vaporize. That means careful use of controlled heat can be used to boil off alcohol from a tincture, leaving only cannabis oil.

Remember: Alcohol is highly flammable—its fumes are explosive. Use a double boiler over an electric hot plate (no flame) to evaporate the alcohol.

Provide ventilation, removing the fumes from the space, or work in an open outdoor space.

Rules for Heating Alcohol

- Avoid open flames.

- Don't use gas stoves or pilot lights.

- Use only electric stoves that have a protected heating section.

- Absolutely no smoking or vaporizing anywhere in the vicinity.

- Work in an extremely well-ventilated area—preferably with a lab ventilator.

- Keep windows open and ventilated using box fans turned to blow air out of the room.

- Wear cotton clothing. Do not wear wool or silk, which produce sparks of static electricity.

Temperature control is critical when reducing tinctures. Never heat a tincture by placing it directly on a burner or stove top, as there will be large differences between the temperature at the bottom and the top. The overheated bottom will produce chemical changes in the extracted oil that will rob it of potent cannabinoids.

Use a double boiler to heat the tincture with less worry. It heats more evenly and the temperature won't exceed 212°F (100°C), the boiling temperature of water. To maintain a lower temperature, use a candy thermometer to check the water in the bottom of the double boiler, or the tincture in the top part. While reducing, stir the tincture frequently with a long spoon or metal kebob skewer.

You can tell when the alcohol has all boiled off because the small alcohol bubbles disappear, leaving the purified oil. The telltale alcohol smell will also disappear.

A basting syringe works well for pulling the oil out of the double boiler. If the oil has particulate matter in it, filter it again through a coffee or lab filter.

This method can also be used to increase the strength of an alcohol tincture without reducing it all the way to oil. Just pull the tincture once the volume has been reduced to the level desired. If you've reduced the volume by half, the resulting tincture will be more than twice as strong as what you started with.

DISTILLING

Wax, dabs, and honey oil are increasingly popular, value-added cannabis products. Each is merely purified extracts of the active cannabinoids and some terpenes found in the marijuana plant. Kief is a close cousin, as is full melt bubble hash. Cannabis oils are made by stripping out the last of the vegetative material, leaving the pure, natural active ingredients.

Many connoisseurs and professionals have turned to purpose-built distillation equipment that uses alcohol or other solvents to extract the essential oils of any herb. The equipment relies on the same basic principal alcohol distillers have used for centuries to produce liquor. Alcohol and other solvents boil at a different temperature from oils or water or other liquids, allowing them to be separated with a cooled condenser. A distilling process uses less alcohol, helps contain the potentially dangerous vapors, and recaptures the alcohol or other solvent for reuse.

Most distilling equipment used with herbs are glass Soxhlet extractors, named for a German agricultural chemist who invented the design in 1879 to separate lipids (such as cannabinoids) from a solid base substance (such as marijuana). Soxhlet extractors use a basket to hold the plant material as heated alcohol or other liquid solvent condenses and drips into it. The warm solvent pulls the oils from the plant material and empties into a siphon arm that returns the oil-laden solvent to the distillation flask, where it is reheated and the process of vaporizing and condensing repeats. This is the same principle that is used in percolator-type coffee pots.

Eden Labs offers modified versions of this design that allow them to operate at lower temperatures and separate out the solvent, leaving just the extracted essence behind. Eden Labs Coldfinger extraction method uses an inverted condenser inside an enclosed glass flask. The condenser is water-cooled and returns the solvent vapors to a liquid state so it can drip down through the plant material and back to the bottom of the flask, where it is reheated.

The resulting tincture can be easily and safely reduced by simply replacing the basket that held the herb with a recovery vessel. The vaporized solvent condenses and drips into the vessel instead of the herb-filled basket, leaving a purified extract in the bottom of the flask. All of this is done at temperatures that stay below 120°F (49°C), so there is little risk of converting the cannabinoids.

GLYCERIN TINCTURES

Alcohol is the standard for making tinctures and it has the advantage of being a great preservative, but for people who cannot tolerate even a drop of alcohol, glycerin tinctures offer an alternative. Some tincture makers use a combination of alcohol and glycerin in their products. Glycerin tinctures are available at many dispensaries, but making your own is not much more involved than making an alcohol tincture. It takes just a few extra steps.

If you have a pure cannabis oil extract, you can make a glycerin tincture by adding a judicious amount of the oil to a bottle of glycerin. Warming it gently (but not too much) and stirring or shaking helps it mix. Pure USP-grade glycerin is inexpensive and available at drug stores everywhere and online.

If making a glycerin tincture from scratch, start by making a carefully strained alcohol tincture. Once you have that, add the alcohol tincture to a comparable amount of glycerin, then evaporate the alcohol. The potency of the glycerin tincture can be adjusted by using either more or less glycerin than the volume of alcohol in the tincture.

One easy method of evaporating the alcohol from the glycerin is to heat it in a double boiler. Measure out the alcohol tincture. To maintain the same strength, add slightly less glycerin, because some of the tincture volume is the cannabis oil. Pour in the alcohol tincture. Using a spoon or spatula, blend them. The larger the surface area of the mixture relative to its depth, the faster alcohol evaporates, so keep the mix limited to a few inches of depth. You'll know when the process is complete because the pan will no longer emit the telltale smell of alcohol. Glycerin tinctures spoil in a few weeks if not refrigerated.

Starting with an alcohol tincture may seem like an unnecessary step, as it is possible to make glycerin tinctures directly. But alcohol is much more efficient at extracting the cannabinoids and other essential oils from marijuana.

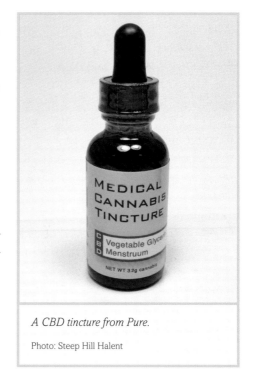

A CBD tincture from Pure.

Photo: Steep Hill Halent

You may encounter people who say you can use your oven to evaporate the alcohol from a tincture, either to make a glycerin tincture or to reduce it to oil. Don't do it. The flash point of pure ethyl alcohol vapor is only about 80°F (27°C), and it only takes 3.3% alcohol vapor volume to produce an explosion. Electric ovens may let you get away with more, but even pot roasts braised in a few cups of wine have been known to end with a bang. Using a double boiler in a well-ventilated area or outdoors is a safe way to evaporate alcohol.

THE EFFECTS AND EFFECTIVENESS OF TINCTURE

Tinctures are administered by dropper under the tongue, or sublingually. The cannabinoids are absorbed by the mucous membranes under the tongue and elsewhere in the mouth and upper throat, releasing them into the bloodstream. Most do not pass through the digestive system, though some can, particularly larger doses, but go directly into the bloodstream. Inhaled cannabis vapor or smoke passes into the bloodstream in the lungs. Direct absorption is an advantage for several reasons: it takes much less time than digestion—it's almost as fast as inhaling, it's easy to titrate because the effects come on rapidly, and the effects are similar to inhaling rather than ingesting.

When substances pass through the digestive system, it takes a minimum of 25 minutes to start feeling their effects, and 45 minutes to an hour before they peak. When there is food in your stomach it takes longer. Swallowed cannabis products pass through the liver which filters what passes into the bloodstream, including some of the cannabinoids. Some of them never reach your bloodstream or your brain. Those cannabinoids that do make it through are subject to the digestive process, which alters THC, so its effects differ from cannabinoids going directly into the bloodstream.

Figuring out tincture dose is much easier than with edibles. The onset of effects is still not nearly as fast as inhalation—which is felt in a matter of seconds—but five minutes after taking the tincture, you can adjust titration. Full effects are felt about 20 minutes after dosage.

Historically, the variable potency of cannabis plants used to make tinctures hindered their use as a modern medicine and contributed to the removal of cannabis from the United States Pharmacopeia. Those two teaspoons that did the trick with one bottle might not in the next batch, making it hard for doctors to prescribe doses with confidence. No one knew what chemicals were in the plant. For the home or artisanal tincture maker, consistency is now less of a challenge. When prepared in one batch or in many small batches from the same plant material, the modern tincture maker has a much easier time creating consistent doses than turn-of-the-century pharmaceutical companies did. Further, tinctures can be tested for potency.

Some people say that tinctures don't affect them much or don't produce the full spectrum of desired effects. Odds are, these people just haven't run across a tincture made properly from cannabis worth extracting. A well-made extract is both a very pleasant and effective way to administer cannabinoids without smoking. It is an excellent choice in no smoking/no vaping situations. You can use cannabis unobtrusively almost anywhere, whether in a theater, traveling or in a park.

Advantages

Cannabis tinctures deliver the effects of smoking with just a short delay. Since they are not burned, no tars or other pyrolytic compounds are inhaled.

Affordable and effective cannabinoid therapy.

Photo: Making You Better Brands

Tinctures are very discreet. The bottle looks like a regular over-the-counter homeopathic medicine. There is no telltale smell to notice as you self-titrate. There is no need to sneak around.

The Proper Dose

Once you have used a particular batch a few times, you will figure out the right dose. Tinctures differ as a result of the cannabinoids and, just as importantly, the terpenes that are present. Plant profiles are part of the equation and processing is the other.

People's tolerance to tinctures differs, just as their tolerance to smoked products varies. Start with small doses, adjusting upward as necessary after waiting at least 45 minutes to gauge effects. Tincture doses typically range between the contents of one dropper (approximately 30–40 drops) and six droppers, but some tinctures are much more potent. Since both tincture potency and people's tolerances differ, there is no way to prescribe a definite dose without knowing the person and the particular tincture.

KIEF TINCTURE

Kief, the sifted glands of marijuana (see chapter 2), is easy to use to make a tincture. Because it is free of most of the vegetative material and is quite concentrated, it makes a very fine extract.

There are several grades of kief. The first sifting is the purest. Each subsequent sift yields a product with more vegetative debris. The first grades are usually used for vaporizing or smoking. The lower grades are best used for cooking and tinctures.

To make a kief tincture, use two grams of kief per ounce of vodka, rum, Everclear, or other alcohol. Place the kief in a jar that can be sealed, or in a blender, and then add the alcohol. Cover tightly and shake the jar or let the blender rip. Let stand at least overnight in a warm, dark place. The mixture can be left longer if desired. Strain the mixture through a paper coffee filter. Transfer the mixture to a clean dropper bottle.

Storage

Label bottles with the date and tincture information to differentiate batches. Tinctures stay potent indefinitely when kept in a cool dark environment, as compared

Store tinctures in dark-colored glass.

Photo: 420 Jars

with glycerine-based tinctures that spoil eventually if not kept refrigerated. The main dangers to a tincture's integrity are heat, light, and oxygen. The best storage for a tincture is in a dark-colored glass container that is sealed and kept in a refrigerator or freezer.

Getting Creative: Variations

While most tinctures use neutral grain spirits or over-proof alcohol, it is possible to use other liquors instead. The higher the proof, the better the cannabinoid-extracting capability. Brandy, bourbon, rum, and other liquors make a more flavorful tincture.

Brandy has a mellow flavor with less burn than pure ethanol, but it is not as effective a solvent because of its lower alcohol content, and its high percentage of water dissolves noncannabinoid, nonactive components such as chlorophyll and other pigments.

A low-tech tincture can be made by just dropping some buds or hash chunks in a bottle of liquor. Within a few weeks most of the cannabinoids will dissolve.

Tinctures can be flavored with honey or other sweeteners. One recipe calls for mixing two parts honey with three parts tincture. Warming the honey thins its consistency, making it easier to mix. Flavor essences are sometimes added to pure alcohol or glycerin tinctures. They are available at specialty cooking shops and on the web.

MULTIHERBAL TINCTURE

If medicinal applications are your interest, then combining a cannabis tincture with other herbs or herbal extracts may be worth experimentation.

Many other herbs can be used with marijuana to create a synergistic effect. Valerian root, passion flower, lemon balm, and marjoram are calming, reduce anxiety, and aid in sleep. Clove extract can be combined with marijuana tincture for an herbal toothache remedy that is rubbed on the gums.

Additional research into herbal combinations is recommended. Consulting an herbalist may yield a multitude of interesting, personalized extracts.

COOKING WITH TINCTURE

Using tinctures is an easy way to cannabinize food. A dropperful in drinks, soups, sauces, or mashed potatoes may be just what the doctor ordered. Tinctures mix well with milk drinks such as shakes, Indian lassi, or hot chocolate. They blend well with sauces and gravies that contain fats and oils.

See chapter 11 for more ideas about how to use tinctures in cooking, or invent recipes of your own. Remember that eating tinctures uses a different process of assimilation, so dosage will have to be reconsidered.

Chapter 10.

Capsules—
Making and Using Canna Caps

We've all been in situations where it's just not cool to smoke. Maybe you've wondered if it were possible to take a marijuana pill. Popping a pill in your mouth with a gulp of water to enjoy the therapeutic and mind-enhancing effects of cannabis would sure be easier and more discreet than firing up a spleef. Turns out you can. Marijuana capsules, also called "maripills" or "canna caps," are very effective and quite easy to make. What's more, they will produce a longer-lasting and somewhat different high than smoking or vaping.

A pill and a pipe won't produce the same effects, even if they contain the same variety

Cannaleve Capsules.

Photo: Nadim Sabella Photography

and amount of marijuana. The digestive process creates somewhat different metabolites from inhaled marijuana, and those have different effects than the smoked form.

One difference is time: how long it takes to be effective and how long the high will last. Take a puff, and the effects are felt within seconds, letting you easily judge how high you're getting. Take a pill, and you won't know for a while. Anything that gets into your system through your stomach takes much longer to be felt, and that can make knowing how much you have on board hard to manage. After 15 or 20 minutes of not feeling much effect, it's easy to think you should just go ahead and pop another canna cap or eat another brownie. Then it starts to really hit you just a few minutes later, but by then you've got a lot more coming. For best results, wait at least an hour before upping the dose.

Just as taking a canna cap or edible takes longer to be felt than inhalation, the effects are also extended. The high from smoking a bowl may have mostly worn off after a couple of hours, but the buzz from a brownie or canna cap will just be getting going. Since digestion takes longer than absorbing through your lungs, that hour or more it takes for your stomach to process what you put in it is like an extended-release for THC and the other cannabinoids. That means that the effects will last at least twice as long, depending somewhat on how much you take.

Those longer-lasting effects make oral ingestion just the ticket for many medical marijuana patients who have trouble sleeping without it or need to go longer between doses for other reasons. Some people prefer the high they get from oral marijuana preparations, and those who use it for chronic pain management often say it works better that way. More of a body high and relaxation is how many describe it, but as with all things marijuana, much of the effect has to do with who is using it and what space they are in.

Cannabinated foods are not always predictable. Canna caps are a more consistent and convenient alternative. Marijuana capsules begin to take effect 30–90 minutes after being eaten, depending on whether you take them with food or on an empty stomach. With capsules, it is easier to monitor the exact amount of cannabis that is being ingested. Psychoactive effects typically last 4 to 8 hours, but the herb's medicinal effects infrequently continue for as long as 12 hours.

Because canna caps allow cannabis to be eaten without food, these capsules give people more choices. When taken on an empty stomach, the high comes on more quickly, and may be more potent, though some people report eating a light meal within an hour helps enhance the effects. When taken following a meal, assimilation is slower, and the effect is mellower but lasts longer. Medical users may find this increased control over effects beneficial.

CANNA CAPS VERSUS MARINOL

Marinol is the brand name given to dronabinol, which consists of synthetic delta-9 THC suspended in a sesame oil base. This is the only cannabis-based medicine currently legal and available by prescription. It's also very expensive.

Some patients experience good results when using Marinol but others find that it produces anxiety or makes them unpleasantly high because it is only the most psychoactive cannabinoid and it lacks cannabidiol (CBD), which counteracts the anxiety-inducing effects of THC.

More importantly for patients seeking the maximum benefit from cannabis, with Marinol you miss out on the "entourage effect" of marijuana's other cannabinoids working together to increase their overall effectiveness. Research has revealed that the aromatic terpenes that give marijuana its distinctive odor make THC three to four times more effective than it is when taken alone. Those other cannabinoids don't just help THC do a better job. They have therapeutic properties of their own, including relieving pain, inflammation, spasm, nausea, and anxiety.

Most modern cannabis contains mostly THC with negligible amounts of other cannabinoids. Some varieties contain CBD, cannabidiol, a nonpsychoactive cannabinoid that has therapeutic properties such as controlling inflammation and anxiety relief. Another cannabinoid, CBG, that is also nonpsychoactive but may have medical effects, is occasionally present.

Since dronabinol does not contain cannabinoids other than THC and does not include terpenes, it is less effective and is more likely to have uncomfortable side effects such as anxiety and paranoia.

Marinol does, of course, have one irrefutable upside—it has passed muster with the Food and Drug Administration and can be prescribed and possessed legally. As a standardized medicine, dosage is exact to a degree that homemade preparations are incapable of matching. Marinol is approved for treating nausea and vomiting resulting from cancer chemotherapy, and for loss of appetite and weight loss related to HIV infection.

Additional cannabis-derived medicines are available by prescription. GW Pharmaceuticals produces Sativex, a dose-controlled plant extract that is half THC, half CBD, in an alcohol-based tincture that is sprayed under the tongue. Sativex is available by prescription for MS and intractable cancer pain in Canada and 23 other countries.

In the meantime, the best option for getting full-spectrum cannabinoids in a discreet and easy-to-use capsule is to make them yourself from quality cannabis. The homemade canna caps discussed in this chapter are made from leaf, trim, or bud, and offer the complete range of therapeutic cannabinoids. Unlike standardized, dosage-controlled pills made by pharmaceutical companies, homemade marijuana capsules will vary in potency from batch to batch, so the dosage should be tested and adjusted each time new capsules are made.

Marijuana capsules can be made either with powdered cannabis or with an oil-based extract. In either case, heat is used to potentiate the THC. Once the material has been processed, it can be packed into gelatin capsules using a large syringe and a small, inexpensive capsule-filling device.

Gelatin capsules and capsule-filling machines are available at many health food stores or online. Capsule-filling machines are small (about the size of a brick) and inexpensive (under $20). They simply hold the gelatin capsule in place, allowing many pills to be made at one time.

If you are a strict vegetarian, gelatin capsules may not be for you as they are made from cows. Vegetarian capsules made of starch are available, but they are inadvisable for this process, because they dissolve when exposed to oil. Ask a salesperson if the vegetarian capsules they offer can tolerate an oil-based filling before purchasing them for canna cap use.

Size #0 capsules are recommended because their small size is not too difficult to swallow. Size #0 can hold 325 milligrams of marijuana preparation. Dosage may vary between 1 and 5 capsules, depending on the potency of the material used. The largest size most people can tolerate is #00 size. The larger size makes preparing them easier, and both the capsules and machines are widely available from health food stores or online. This size has a capacity of 650 milligrams. Usually 1–2 pills at this size comprise a sufficient dose.

HOW TO MAKE CANNA CAPS

Canna caps can be made from leaf and trim only, bud only, or a leaf/bud combination. No matter what is used, it is necessary to process the plant material before filling capsules. There are three basic ways cannabis can be capsulized: as just dry powder, as powder mixed with an oil, or as an oil extract of the cannabis.

All three methods need the plant material to be heated a bit to "decarboxylate" it, a chemical process that changes the cannabinoids found in the plant—THCA and CBDA, which are nonpsychoactivce—to the active form by releasing COOH from the molecule. That process happens naturally when you smoke or vaporize marijuana, but for preparations you swallow, it needs to be done separately.

Mild heat, about 100°F (38°C), also helps the cannabinoids bind to the oil, if that's the method you're using. Packing the capsules with a mixture of marijuana and oil makes it easier for the body to digest and utilize the herb. Whole plant material contains not only the bulbous THC-containing glands but also the microscopic—and sharp—hairs on which they rest. Oil and heat soften these spiky hairs, making them less irritating to the stomach.

The cannabinoids and other essential oils that produce marijuana's effects are soluble in fats, oils, and alcohol. They are not soluble in water. Gelatin caps hold nonaqueous liquids such as oil and alcohol, but they dissolve when filled with water. Luckily, marijuana is mixed with these liquids, not water.

Some people find that, even after processing, they have trouble digesting pills that use leaf material. If this is the case, try using hash or kief. Both kief and hash contain much less vegetative matter. The tiny hairs from the vegetative matter are most likely the culprits in digestive complaints.

If that's a problem, just make your canna caps with the strained oil method described below.

Equipment and Ingredients

- Cooking oil (coconut, olive, or canola)

- Plant material (bud, leaf, trim, or a combination)

- Food processor or flour mill (when leaf/trim is used)

- Clean or unused coffee grinder

- Flour sifter (optional)

- Crockpot, double boiler, or small saucepan

- Cookie sheet

- Candy thermometer (optional)

- Gelatin capsules

- Capsule-filling machine

- Tamping tool if using vegetative material (machine may come with one; otherwise, the head of a nail works well)

- Large syringe (if using oil only)

- Paper cone coffee filter (if using oil only)

Processing Leaf and Bud for Capsules

Clean the leaf, trim, or cured bud carefully before starting the capsule-making process. Make sure there are no small stems in your material. Kief and hash are already well suited to capsule making, though caution should be used with dosage, as the end product may be very potent.

The material should be very dry before beginning this process. Spread the material on a cookie sheet and place it in an oven at 100°F (38°C) for an hour to remove the last remnants of moisture and decarboxylate it.

MARIJUANA PILLS

Ask Ed

Ed:

Is there a way to make marijuana pills or capsules? I reek after smoking and I don't like to cook the stuff. When I consume marijuana I have a deeper high. Another reason why I want to consume rather than smoke it is to give my lungs a well-needed rest. Do you have any recipes or ideas?

Budd,
Internet

Budd:

My late friend Tom flowers used to use maricaps for his severe arthritis. He bought size #0 capsules and a filler holder that holds them upright. He used high-grade trim that was well dried and powdered fine in a coffee grinder. The powder was mixed with a few lecithin granules and enough olive oil to make a thick paste. Then the caps were filled and kept in the refrigerator or freezer until used.

Each cap held about a third of a gram of high-quality trim. Tom used them for relief of arthritic pain. Three or four caps on an empty stomach were quite potent. The advantage of caps is that you don't have to eat to use them.

The lecithin is added to help emulsify the THC. It's quite possible that a glass of milk (soy is okay), laden with emulsifiers, might help with the high.

Chop the material into a fine powder or flour using a coffee grinder or blender. This processing generates clouds of cannabis dust that contain many glands that can be retained by letting the dust settle before you open the top.

If the material contains a lot of leaf, follow the coffee-grinding step with an additional pass through a flour sifter. This last step makes the material finer and more consistent by separating out any large pieces.

Don't skimp on material. It is always better to have more marijuana powder than you plan to use, so if too much oil is added accidentally, a little more powder can also be added to reach the right consistency. Extra capsule powder can be stored in the freezer. The refrigerator is also adequate. Cold, dark, and oxygen-free conditions preserve marijuana's potency and protect it against molds or bacteria.

Making the Filling

Pure Canna Oil Caps

Some of the best canna caps are made with strained coconut oil cannabis preparations. Coconut oil works well because it is a soft solid at room temperature, is readily available in pure organic forms from health food stores, and is almost 100% nonhydrogenated fat, so it's healthful in its own right. Olive oil is another popular medium because it is healthful and stable at room temperature.

To heat the oil and cannabis, a double boiler or Crockpot works well and helps ensure you don't overheat it. As with other marijuana preparations, keeping heat low is key to preserving the cannabinoids that will vaporize and escape when temperatures get above 280°F (138°C).

Calculating Quantities

Capsule machines may make 24, 50, or 100 capsules at a time. Size #0 capsules hold 0.3 grams, and #00 capsules hold 0.6 grams. The amount it takes to fill 50 capsules is 15 grams (about a half-ounce) for size #0, and 30 grams (about 1 ounce) for #00.

Place the desired amount of oil in a double boiler or Crockpot. A small frying pan or saucepan will also work if care is taken to keep the temperature at 100°F (38°C). (That's where the candy thermometer comes in.) Once the oil has warmed, add the ground marijuana, stirring to coat the material thoroughly.

If you are straining out the plant material to make oil-only capsules, the longer you let the mixture heat, the better. It takes a while for all of the cannabinoids and plant oils to bind to the coconut oil. Half an hour is the minimum, an hour captures almost all the THC, and six hours is great for the obsessive. Using a Crockpot or other slow cooker saves you constantly monitoring the heat. The oil-to-powder ratio varies between 3–8 tablespoons per ounce because leaf and bud absorb oil in different quantities. Use just enough oil to make the material stick together in a dry paste-like consistency, particularly if you are using an oil other than coconut that is fluid at room temperature. Too much oil makes filling the capsules more difficult. More powder should be added if the mixture seems too oily.

The mixture should keep the same dark green color it started with. If the material turns brown, it has burned, which is unfortunate. This material has lost most of its value. You should start over rather than continuing with this material.

If you are using a saucepan or skillet and want capsules that contain all the plant material, heat the oil using a candy thermometer to monitor the exact temperature. Once the temperature reaches 100°F (38°C), remove the pan from the stove and add the plant material to reach the proper consistency. The mixture can be encapsulated when it has cooled to room temperature (below 90°F [32°C]).

Filling the Capsules

Capsule machines have a platform with holes. The bottom of the capsule shells fit into this platform. The process for filling the capsules is only slightly different for using just the oil or the full plant-oil mix.

For oil-only capsules, heat the mix until it is liquid rather than viscous, fill a large syringe or baster with the oil, then inject it into the capsules one by one. Don't let the mixture get too cool before filling the capsules, or getting it into them will be difficult if not impossible. If it does harden, just gently reheat it to the point of turning to liquid.

For capsules that use the full oil-plant mix, use a spreading card to distribute the oil mixture over the capsule-filling device. Tamp the mixture down into the capsules. Repeat the process until they are completely filled. If your capsule-making kit did not come with a tamper, sterilize a nail with the right-sized head and use it.

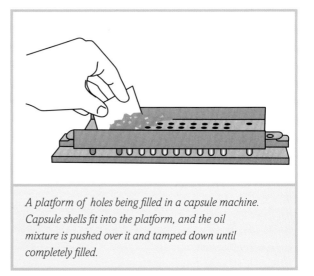

A platform of holes being filled in a capsule machine. Capsule shells fit into the platform, and the oil mixture is pushed over it and tamped down until completely filled.

Storage

Keep canna caps in a sealed, dark glass bottle or jar. They have a shelf life of only a few weeks at room temperature, but in the refrigerator, they keep for months. They can also be stored long term in a freezer.

- Gelatin caps are derived from animal products. Vegetarian capsules can be used, but some types dissolve when oil is used in the filling. Before buying vegetarian capsules, ask the salesperson if they can be filled with an oil-based mixture.

- It is a good idea to process a little extra powdered material. Then the material-to-oil ratio can be adjusted if too much oil is accidentally mixed in.

- When heating plant material for the capsules, heat it in a double boiler rather than on a stove top to assure keeping a low temperature. THC starts to vaporize at just over 280°F (138°C). Some terpenes are volatile at 70°F (21°C). If using a burner set it at a very low temperature to avoid ruining the plant material's psychoactive and therapeutic properties. A Crockpot or other slow cooker set on low works well.

- Bud absorbs more oil than leaf material. The amount of oil needed may depend on the ratio of leaf to bud, the type of oil used, and how dry the plant material is.

- Marijuana varieties differ in potency and cannabinoid content. Different strains produce different highs and medicinal qualities. Likewise, using different ratios of trim, bud, leaf, or kief affects potency. Reassess dosage when a new combination of plant material is used.

USING KIEF

Kief offers a cleaner alternative to powdered leaf or bud especially for those who find plant material hard to digest. Kief dissolves easily when mixed in warm oil. It does not have a dark green color when mixed and heated because it doesn't contain plant matter. Kief is more concentrated than bud so a kief-packed pill will be more potent. Try size #0 capsules when using kief because the dosing size is smaller.

DOSAGE

As with all marijuana products, the right dosage depends on the potency of the herb, how you prepare it, and the person taking it. Dosage varies from person to person and from batch to batch, but it usually ranges between one to five size #0 capsules or one to two #00 capsules.

When capsules are made using only powdered bud, they are more potent than a bud/leaf or leaf/trim mixture. Likewise, kief, which is a concentrated form of marijuana, has a higher potency, and the dosage should be lowered.

Canna caps can be taken at any time, but just like marijuana foods, results depend in part on whether they are eaten on an empty or full stomach. When taken on an empty stomach, the onset of effects is more rapid, and the high may be more intense. Eating food right after the pills are taken may mitigate the potency and delivery, though some say a light meal within an hour enhances the high. If canna caps are taken after a meal, the effects will come on more slowly and the high may be milder. As always, effects will also differ from person to person, so start with small amounts and give it at least 90 minutes to take effect.

Chapter 11.

Edibles—

Preparation, Recipes, Usage

Eating foods made with marijuana is a healthy and popular way to use it. The effects of eating marijuana are longer lasting, making it a great choice for a constant, long-lasting buzz. It is a preferred choice for people who use marijuana for long-lasting medical relief. Marijuana-based foods range from confections and beverages to main courses. Consuming cannabis is more discreet than smoking, since there is no telltale flame, smoke, or odor.

Aunt Sandy's Munchie Bars.

Photo: Joe Burull

COOKING

Cannabinated foods are a common therapeutic alternative for medical marijuana use. If you are unfamiliar with an ingestible product's effects, it is best to use too little rather than too much. You can always eat more, but you have to wait out the effects of too large a dose, an unpleasant experience, but not dangerous. Your body will continue to function, and you will come down within a few hours.

Preparing the Ingredients

The secret to creating tasty and effective cannabis food lies in infusing a cooking ingredient, such as an oil, butter, milk, or flour, with the herb's active ingredients. Marijuana can also be used raw or dried, from leaf to kief, in a variety of foods and beverages. Once you've mastered enriching the ingredients, it's easy to turn your favorite recipes into cannabis treats. A few recipes are included, but cannabis cookbooks such as *Aunt Sandy's Medical Marijuana Cookbook* and cannabis cooking websites provide many more.

HOW IT WORKS

Food-Cannabis Chemistry

The first time I got high from consuming cannabis, my host heated tomato sauce from a jar and added two teaspoons of ground trim that was mixed with a tablespoon of olive oil. We were high by the time we stopped eating, stoned within the hour, and didn't come down until hours later. Obviously, cooking with marijuana is not rocket science.

Still, following a few simple procedures in preparing the herb will result in a better dish and a more enjoyable experience. An important point to remember is that THC and other cannabinoids are not water soluble. Good cannabis consumables couple the plant material with an ingredient that can dissolve the cannabinoids, such as alcohol, oil, butter, or fat-containing milk products. Lecithin, an emulsifier that allows oil to mix but not dissolve in water, is sometimes used as an alternative carrier or in conjunction with solvents such as oil or alcohol.

Mild heat plays an important role in cannabis cooking. THC starts out in the plant as THC acid (THCA). THCA is much less psychoactive than THC. Chemically, it is THC with an attached carbonate molecule (COOH; or carbon, oxygen, oxygen, hydrogen). It detaches easily with heat, and evaporates as water vapor and carbon dioxide, converting THCA to its psychoactively effective cousin, THC. This process, called decarboxylation, happens naturally when marijuana is smoked or vaporized. For use in food stuffs, heat must be applied either before or during cooking.

THC has a boiling temperature of 314.6°F (157°C). Once it reaches or passes this temperature, it evaporates and forms tiny liquid drops as it cools. Prolonged heat also chemically alters the THC. Heating marijuana for 30 minutes at 250°F (121°C) converts almost all the THCA to THC; the THC rapidly converts to the much more sedative and less psychoactive CBN. To get the most out of your marijuana ingredients, keep a close eye on the cooking temperatures and times and modify some techniques.

Extend the high with Kannabliss by Couchlock. Drink before using cannabis for a longer-lasting buzz, even with low-grade weed.

Photo: Couchlock

The oven temperature for baking is typically set at 350°F (177°C). This won't evaporate off all the THC because, while the oven may be 350°F (177°C), only the surface of the batter reaches this temperature. If you've ever roasted a Thanksgiving turkey, you know that even if the oven is set to 350°F (177°C), the thermometer inserted into the bird only has to hit just under 200°F (93°C) to call the bird done—and a turkey cooks for hours. Baking temperatures indicate oven temperatures, not the food temperature.

Stove-top cooking must be closely monitored to avoid evaporating the THC. Frying and sautéing food reaches temperatures as high as 400°F (204°C), well above THC's boiling point. At this temperature, the cannabinoids quickly escape as vapor, leaving little to consume. To prevent this add grass, hash, kief, tincture, oil, or a butter/oil-THC mix directly to the sauté only when the dish is almost done.

When is Cannabis Edible?

If you've ever eaten raw buds or other plant material, you know that it can give you a buzz, but it is neither a very efficient nor an appetizing method of consumption, although it isn't dangerous. Marijuana isn't called herb for nothing; in cooking, it is used as an herb. It can be added directly to foods such as soups or stews, but some people find the green chlorophyll flavor objectionable. If the pieces are too big, people often find the texture chewy, like an herb leaf.

Eating food made with hash or kief is different than eating raw vegetation. Kief consists of the THC-containing glands, which are a fine golden to green powder depending on quality. Hash results when kief is pressed under warm conditions. The gland heads break and the oils emerge, forming a dense, sticky mass. Hash eating has a long history, both as a food ingredient and as a stand-alone edible. Kief is rapidly gaining popularity because it's easy to use in foods. Just sprinkle it on or in the food shortly before eating.

The first time I ingested kief, it was mixed with olive oil and stuffed into a size #00 capsule that was kept in the refrigerator. One was enough for the evening. At times that evening, I thought I was living in slow motion.

Eating kief or hash alone occasionally results in a mildly uncomfortable stomach. However, they are excellent choices for enhancing food and they have little effect on the digestive system. They are especially good as direct additives in dishes that already contain oil. Both kief and hash are concentrates so you only need to use a little. Make sure it is thoroughly mixed into the dish to avoid "hot spots."

Kief Shaker

For convenience keep a "kief shaker" handy in the kitchen. Salt shakers work great. Place a few grains of dry, uncooked rice in the shaker to absorb moisture, keeping the kief dry and ready to shake. The shaker is easily used during cooking or to "season" food once it's prepared. Adding some post-preparation kief is the best way to make a marijuana sauté because it avoids the high heat that would vaporize the cannabinoids. Golden kief is a fine condiment for pizza, just like parmesan cheese.

Ask Ed

Ed:
I like to eat marijuana-laced food, but I don't like the taste of it.
Is there any way to avoid getting that funky green flavor?

Lauren
Nova Scotia

Lauren:

Eliminate the pigments and chlorophyll that give marijuana-laced food its "green" taste.

One way to do this is to use kief rather than marijuana.

Another method is to clean the butter or oil before cooking with it. Chlorophyll and other pigments are water soluble so they can be separated from the butter. Melt the marijuana butter, add water, and let it simmer for a few minutes. Cool it. The fatty part of the butter or the oil, which contains the cannabinoids, rises to the top. The water, with the pigments, is underneath. Remove the top part and throw the water away. The process doesn't eliminate all the pigments, but it does reduce their presence.

ASSIMILATION AND DOSAGE

What to Know Before You Start

Ingesting food or beverages infused with marijuana or an extract is a different experience than inhaling it or using a tincture. The cannabinoids, marijuana's active ingredients, are metabolized differently when digested than when inhaled, altering their effects. Ingesting, there is not an immediate rush. Instead the time to onset is much longer, and the effects are longer lasting. The sensation begins gradually a half-hour to an hour and a half after ingestion. The high lasts between three and six hours, depending on dose and speed of digestion.

Getting the dose right is much more important when ingesting than inhaling. Inhaled marijuana creates effects within seconds that are fully felt within a few minutes, making it easy to self-titrate—that is, to achieve the desired level of high or medication. Marijuana edibles take much longer for the effects to be felt, and they come on gradually, making it harder to judge if the dose is right.

The amount of food you've eaten, how the food was prepared, and the cannabis's potency all affect how your body processes the THC and other cannabinoids, which affects the length and intensity of the high. Eating cannabis is more likely to produce a psychedelic experience than inhaling. Inexperienced people trying ingestion should use caution and have a buddy nearby.

Alcohol is the most rapid form of delivering cannabinoids. Sublingually (drops under the tongue), it is directly absorbed through mucus membranes in the mouth and throat, taking five minutes or less. It is also the shortest lasting. The high and other effects are similar to inhaling because the THC and other cannabinoids and terpenes pass through the mucus membrane directly into the bloodstream, similar to how the cannabinoids in smoke pass into the bloodstream in the lungs. In a mixed drink it reaches the stomach, where there is a slight delay before it enters the bloodstream. The onset is rapid because alcohol, a small molecule, quickly passes through the stomach lining.

Ingested THC is slowly metabolized as it passes through the digestive system. The cannabinoids are delivered to the bloodstream over a longer period of time, so the effects last longer. THC in butter takes the longest to get into the bloodstream and has the longest-lasting effects.

The fats in milk products absorb THC and other cannabinoids and emulsify them because of the lecithin they contain. India's Bhang (marijuana) Lassi drinks are dairy based. Dairy and soy milk contain lecithin, an emulsifier that breaks oil into small bits so they remain suspended in water. Lecithin also speeds the absorption of cannabinated milk products, decreasing absorption time better than oil or butter bases alone.

Since the effects of smoking are quick and are felt all at once, a common experience of novice marijuana eaters is to think that the first mild effects of an edible, felt after 30 minutes or so, are all they are going to get. Most of the effects are still on the way, but they double the dose. When the high starts to reach its peak an hour later, it will be much more than expected.

A similar mistake can be made if you don't know the edible's potency. Just because it tastes great doesn't mean having a few extra bites is a good idea. Relying only on the experience of others is not wise either, as the effects of edibles differ from person to person. Use caution when consuming any cannabis food product for the first time, even if you are a veteran smoker. Choose modest portions.

As a host, monitor the amount of cannabinized food guests consume. Never give or let people consume spiked food without their knowledge.

Don't underestimate the temptation of the munchies. Prepare for them by having something other than cannabis treats to snack on. This is especially a good idea when making a dessert dish or something for a group gathering. Everyone can continue to snack without going overboard.

Treating Overdose—Too Much of a Good Thing

Marijuana's toxicity level is so low that it remains undetermined. Statistics suggest that a person would have to ingest several thousand times the typical amount of cannabis to reach a level that interferes with bodily functions. Putting this in perspective, coffee has fatal effects at 100 times the typical amount. Hence the statistic: No deaths result from marijuana overdose.

Eating marijuana is the easiest way to get too high. The delayed effect and gradual onset make dosage harder to gauge and can lead to consuming more than necessary for the desired effect. This can be an unpleasant experience, partly because the difference in effects between inhaled cannabinoids and cannabinoids metabolized in the digestive system creates unfamiliar effects. Avoid this problem by using restraint in eating cannabinized foods until you determine proper dosage. It is always possible to eat more, but once it's in your stomach, there's no going back.

Edibles have less "plateau effect" than smoking. People reach a certain high when smoking, then stay about that level even if they continue to smoke. That effect doesn't occur with ingested cannabis. Most of the time, when people have eaten too much they will be excited and a little hyper for an hour or so. Then they'll tire and fall into a deep sleep. This is usually the best option for dealing with an excessive dose.

If you eat yourself beyond your comfort limit there are a few things that can be done:

- Remember that you are in no physical danger, even though you may be experiencing a distorted reality. Although the high will last several hours, the most intense feelings occur within an hour after the effects begin. Those intense feelings will soon fade.

- Remember that these sensations will all pass in a little while.

- Sit or lie down and try to relax. If you are lying down you cannot fall so any feeling of spinning, imbalance, or dizziness will not result in injury. Keeping your eyes open may relieve some of these symptoms.

- Remember the anxiety is all in your head. There is another reality out there.

- You may experience chills. Treat them by keeping warm.

PREPARING THE HERB

The guidelines for preparing marijuana for use in cooking do not differ much from preparing it for smoking. Remove seeds and stems.

Before using any marijuana, inspect it closely for mold. Gray mold or bud rot usually appears in humid climates while the plant is still growing and is seen close to the stem where moisture can get trapped. Other molds result from improper drying, curing, or storage. Some molds produce black or brown spots. Moldy pot is not suitable for any use because it may contain toxins. Anaerobic bacteria can be detected by the ammonia smell they release.

Bud bits, dried trim, and leaf can all be used, alone or in combination, to make cannabis butter, cooking oil, milks, or flour. The marijuana should be dry to the point of being crispy before using. To eliminate any residual moisture, spread it on a cookie sheet and place it in a 90°F–100°F (32°C –38°C) oven. An electric food dehydrator set on low is useful for decarboxylating the leaves. Once the material is brittle to the touch, it's ready to use.

All the glands are on the surface of the leaves, so they do not have to be ground to make contact with butter, cooking oil, or alcohol. When making these building blocks for cannabis cooking, most people filter out the marijuana plant material once the cannabinoids have been extracted. Leaving the leaf material whole makes filtering it much easier.

Some recipes use marijuana flour. Prepare it by removing all the stems, large and small. Grind the material to a powder using a food processor, blender, or coffee grinder. After operating, don't open the grinding device immediately; wait a couple of minutes for the gland dust to settle.

USING HASH, KIEF, OR HASH OIL IN FOOD

While this chapter focuses on using leaf and trim material to make ingredients, hash, kief, and hash oil are easy-to-use, excellent ingredients for cooking. They concentrate the cannabinoid dose without the vegetation, resulting in a cleaner, less "green" taste.

Using concentrate oil is a good way to have dosage consistency when making edibles. Dabber's Delight is a CBD-rich concentrate that is orally safe.

Not much concentrate is needed for each portion, making it even more important that these ingredients are mixed thoroughly to keep portions uniform. Alcohol and butane solvents remaining from processing hash oil evaporate quickly when exposed to cooking heat.

Hash, kief, and hash oil need some preparation before they are used in cooking. Grind, shave, or chop the hash to a fine consistency using a coffee grinder or blender. Then add cooking oil or alcohol and blend into a mush or slush using a blender or by placing everything in a jar with a tight cover and shaking it.

JUICING

Many people juice raw marijuana for its health benefits. Juicing fresh buds and leaves lets you ingest large amounts of THC in its nonpsychoactive acid form, THCA, and CBDA, the acid form of CBD, which has anti-inflammatory, anti-oxidant, and cancer-fighting properties, as well as stimulating effects on the immune system. The juice also contains terpenes, which have mood-altering and therapeutic qualities. It doesn't produce the high of decarboxylated bud, but the terpenes produce noticeable effects.

The therapeutic potential of raw cannabis has not been studied in clinical trials, but reports of individuals achieving good results, such as Dr. William Courtney's wife Kristen, who, attacked by Lupus, improved dramatically after treatment with the raw juice. Dr. Courtney recommends using it in large quantities, as much as 100 times greater than you would smoke. Many other people also report medical improvement for a variety of chronic physical ailments. Effects may be immediate or take weeks of treatment. Drinking large quantities of marijuana juice as a dietary supplement may be rough on kidneys and gallbladders, so it is not recommend for people with conditions affecting those organs.

Commercial juicing devices such as wheat grass juicers are the most efficient. Juice is made by dropping fresh-from-the-plant bud, trim, and leaf in the blender, then straining it using a sieve or squeezing it through cheesecloth to eliminate the drained vegetative material. If you are not averse to alcohol, soak the solids in grain alcohol or high-proof vodka, then squeeze it out to remove the remaining cannabinoids. The juice tastes bitter, so most users mix it into other drinks.

Soaking leaf or bud in water removes dirt or other environmental elements from the plant surfaces. Check the material for mold and mildew. Without the heat of cooking or combustion to inactivate them, these unwanted materials flow with the juice.

You can preserve the juice by freezing it. Fill ice cube trays with your fresh juice, freeze it, then use as desired.

USING TINCTURES IN FOOD

Tinctures are ready to consume so they can be dropped (added to food using a dropper) on baked goods, salad dressings, beverages, or other foods shortly before serving. Make sure to measure dosage because it's easy to overdo the drops and they are more potent than cannabinated alcohol, butter, milk, or oil.

MAKING BASIC INGREDIENTS

Potency: Plant Material Ratios

When using a cannabinated ingredient its potency and the strength that you want the food to have determine appropriate serving size.

The potency of the plant material used usually varies between batches. If you can have it tested for potency at one of the cannabis labs you can standardize dosage. For instance if the material has 5% THC and a previous batch had 4%, divide 4 by 5 to determine 0.8, a fifth less. If analysis isn't available, try testing it subjectively by smoking a tiny bit of the material. Comparing it with material from the previous batch gives you a good subjective comparison.

Regardless of the testing method used, consider the serving size before starting a recipe: Do you want to get high off of a teaspoon of butter spread on toast? Do you want to be able to eat a WHOLE cookie without going overboard? Adjust your recipes accordingly.

Label Your Ingredients

Anytime you make a cannabis cooking ingredient, label it prominently with something that distinguishes it from nonmedicated oils.

Steep Hill Halent Lab protects public health by providing infrastructure and analytical services.

CANNA OIL PREPARATION AND RECIPES

- 1 oz dry leaf, ½ oz trim, or ¼–⅛ oz bud
- 1 pint (16 oz) oil

Yields 8 Servings

Cannabis-infused cooking oil is versatile and easily stored. Keep it in the refrigerator to prevent deterioration. Unlike butters and milk, canna oil can be used in vegan recipes. Canola, coconut, olive, and flaxseed oils are excellent choices for cannabis cooking oil. They all dissolve cannabinoids and aid its transfer through the digestive system to the bloodstream.

Once an oil has been infused with cannabinoids, it can be substituted for nonmedicated oils in most recipes. Don't fry with it or use it for high-temperature sautés because the cannabinoids start evaporating during high-heat cooking. They'll be gone before the food hits the plate. Cannabinoids will not boil off, because the water temperature only reaches 212°F (100°C).

Photo: Joe Burull

Make herbal butters, oils, tinctures, and more with the MagicalButter extractor. Just add the ingredients and the machine extracts. It decarboxylates the THCA to THC, potentiating it.

Photo: MagicalButter

The easiest way to make cannabinated oil is to add marijuana to the oil and let it sit a few weeks. Strain (or not) before using.

Apply a low heat to the oil and cannabis mixture using a low burner, double boiler, or Crockpot to help the THC dissolve faster. Don't heat the oil and cannabis directly in a pan on the stove top because the cannabinoids are easily degraded.

To make infused oil, use a ratio of two cups of vegetable oil to one ounce of leaf/trim. Make it stronger or weaker by reducing or increasing the amount of oil or increasing/decreasing the amount of plant material. Substituting ground bud, kief, or hash for trim results in a stronger oil.

1. Measure the cooking oil and add it to the slow cooker. Set the cooker on low.

2. Once the oil has warmed, add the marijuana.

3. Heat the mixture to 125°F–150°F (52°C–66°C) for 6 hours, stirring hourly.

4. Let cool. This takes a while.

5. Pour into a bottle, filtering the oil with a funnel lined with cheesecloth or a coffee filter.

6. Label the oil.

7. Refrigerate to protect the cannabinoids from degrading.

To reclaim every last bit of oil return the oily plant material to the slow cooker, cover with water, stir, and cook on low for an additional hour or two. Strain into a separate, open-top container, then place in the freezer. Once the water freezes, pour off the remaining oil.

Use cannabinated cooking oil in recipes that list oil as an ingredient. Sauces and salad dressings are ideal because the temperature never rises above water's boiling point, far below THC's boiling point.

Make your favorite tomato soup or gazpacho, then drizzle a little cannabinated olive oil on top before serving. Brush some on toasted baguette slices, rub with raw garlic, then add some diced tomatoes and basil to make a killer bruschetta. Or just put some cannabinated olive oil in a shallow bowl, add a smidge of balsamic vinegar and salt, and dip your favorite bread.

One of the best canna olive oil entrée options is fresh pesto pasta. It only takes ten minutes to make if you have a food processor, and the garlic content and nuttiness complement cannabis flavors nicely.

Pesto

Ingredients

- ½ cup cannabinated olive oil
- 2 cups fresh basil leaves
- ⅓ cup pine nuts (cashews can be substituted)
- 2–3 garlic cloves
- Salt and black pepper
- ⅓ cup walnuts or parmesan cheese (optional)

1. Place basil, garlic, and pine nuts or cashews in the food processor and give it a few pulses to mix.

2. Add ⅓ cup walnuts or parmesan cheese.*

3. With the food processor on a low setting to reduce splatter, slowly add the canna olive oil.

4. The pesto will coat the sides, so stop every once in a while and use a rubber spatula to scrape it back down so it mixes evenly.

5. Add salt and freshly ground pepper to taste.

Walnuts taste similar to the cheese but keep the recipe vegan.

Serve with pasta or as pizza sauce, with polenta, or spread it on toasted baguette slices.

Simple Salad Dressing

Ingredients

- ⅓ cup cannabinated olive oil
- 3 tablespoons balsamic vinegar
- 2 teaspoons Dijon mustard
- ½ teaspoon kosher or sea salt
- Pinch of black pepper
- Pinch of vegetable lecithin granules (optional)

Photo: Joe Burull

Directions

Combine ingredients in a shallow bowl and whisk together, or simply add to a bottle and shake. Add to salad. If refrigerating any excess canna dressing, label appropriately.

Lecithin slows the oil/vinegar separation.

Yields 4 Servings

CANNA BUTTER THREE WAYS

There are many techniques for making canna butter. Three basic methods are described here. Workable cooking times vary but shouldn't exceed the longest times suggested.

Slow Cooker Method

The slow cooker method is the easiest, so that's the one we'll start with. Slow cookers and Crockpots are inexpensive new and are readily available used. They are perfect for making cannabis-enriched foods because they are specifically designed to simmer foods at low temperatures for long periods of time. Anything made in a slow cooker is a good candidate for cannabinating. It is also the lowest-hassle tool for making canna butter.

Stove-top herbal extractors turn flowers into cannabis butter in less than 10 minutes. The MOTA POT is an affordable, easy-to-use appliance that controls the dose to produce the perfect amount of infused butter.

Photo: Extracting Innovations

Equipment and Ingredients

- Slow cooker (Crockpot)
- 1 oz dry leaf, ½ oz trim, or ¼–⅛ oz bud (Smaller amount: ⅛ oz leaf in 2 oz butter)
- 1 lb butter
- 1 quart water
- Stirring utensil
- Metal strainer or mesh sieve and cheesecloth (or new pair of nylon panty hose)

Note that this recipe is for one pound of butter, but you can as easily make less or much more. Adapt the ratio of one ounce of weed to one pound of butter depending on the quality of the marijuana being used and the desired potency of the canna butter.

Measure the butter, water, and plant material, and place in the slow cooker.

Set the temperature on low, which should be no more than 200°F (93°C). You can check it with a meat or candy thermometer.

Cover and let simmer 1–4 hours, stirring hourly.

When done, freeze. The butter will rise to the top and is easily peeled from the water/grass mixture which contains no THC and can be tossed. It contains much of the chlorophyll and other plant flavors from the butter.

Warm the butter so it flows freely. Strain into a clean bowl using a mesh sieve, cheesecloth, or a pair of panty hose. If plant particles get through the sieve, refilter through fine cheesecloth. Squeeze as much melted butter out of the plant material as possible by pressing on the filter with a spoon or squeezing out the cheesecloth or panty hose. Pour into a container for storage.

LONG-TERM STORAGE

Canna butter can be safely frozen indefinitely and will store in the refrigerator as long as regular butter. To make easily apportioned canna butter cubes pour the strained, melted butter into ice cube trays and place in the freezer.

The Stove-Top Water Method (Yields 8 Servings)

One tablespoon of butter is to be the serving size. Making it that potent requires more plant material than butter. The solution is to add two cups of water for each cup of butter. Boil the mixture for an hour. The water absorbs the green pigments and flavors, while the fatty part of the butter absorbs the cannabinoids. Strain out the plant material, then cool the mixture in the freezer. When the butter solidifies remove it from the top of the pot.

This method works well for making high-potency butter. The recipe below uses the standard one ounce to one pound ratio, but this method lets you use more weed or less butter, making a more potent concoction.

Equipment and Ingredients

- A large pot
- 1 oz dry leaf, ½ oz trim, or ¼–⅛ oz bud
- ¼ lb butter
- 4 cups water
- Metal strainer or mesh sieve and/or cheesecloth (or new pair of nylon panty hose)
- Stirring utensil

Bring the water to a boil. Add the butter and plant material. Lower the heat to maintain a low boil. Cook for an hour. Stir regularly. Add more water as the level drops.

Freeze the mixture and peel the butter off the top. Toss the water/leaf mixture, which contains no THC. Heat the butter until it flows freely. Strain the mixture into a bowl using a mesh sieve, cheesecloth, or a pair of panty hose. Store in a refrigerator or freezer.

The Skillet Method

The skillet method is a quick and easy alternative to make small batches of canna butter.

Equipment and Ingredients

- A skillet, sauté, or frying pan
- Dry plant material
- Butter
- Metal strainer, mesh sieve, and/or cheesecloth
- Stirring utensil

Place the desired amount of butter and plant material in a skillet, sauté, or frying pan. To extract as much THC as possible without losing it to evaporation, keep the heat very low—just high enough to melt it. If the butter starts to bubble, it is too hot. Simmer the marijuana in the melted butter for 30 minutes. Strain and use.

PANTY HOSE STRAINING

Some chefs swear by panty hose for straining out plant material from oils or butters. Panty hose are less likely than pastry cloth or cheesecloth to rip when squeezed hard, and they don't absorb any oil or butter.

Pour the butter/plant mixture, warm enough to flow freely, into a leg of clean, unused panty hose held over a clean container. Having another person hold the panty hose or pour is helpful. If you are working solo, just stretch the panty hose over the bowl so one leg is inside. Pour the mix into the panty hose–lined bowl. Then carefully lift the panty hose out of the bowl and let the contents filter into the bowl. Wring out any remaining liquid.

Changing the Ingredients

Using Hash or Kief Instead of Marijuana

It is really easy to make canna butter using hash and kief. Just blend the desired amount with melted butter. Cooking time is minimal, since the cannabinoids have already been separated from the plant material. No water or straining is necessary since there isn't much extraneous plant material. A slow cooker or double boiler ensures that you don't overheat it, but a pan on a stove top works as long as the heat is kept low. Once the kief or hash dissolves into the melted butter, it is ready to use.

REFILTER FOR FLAVOR

If a butter recipe has been prepared using a nonwater method and is found to be particularly harsh tasting, it is not too late to get the advantages of water. Heat the butter and add twice as much water as there is butter. Bring the water to a low boil and cook for 15–30 minutes. Some of the harsh flavors and color will migrate from the butter to the water. Once it cools, the hardened butter will float on top of the water.

Using Margarine or Coconut Oil

Butter is the choice of most bakers because of its flavor and ease of use, but vegan chefs use margarine or unrefined coconut oil. Margarine, like butter, is a combination of fatty oils and water. Both butter and margarine contain lecithin, which helps oils mix with water in suspensions. Most brands of margarine contain more water than butter does. The water boils off during cooking, leaving less final product. Figure that for every pound (2 cups) of margarine you start with, the end result will be about ¾ lb (1½ cups). Coconut oil works well as a butter substitute be-

RICE CRISPY TREATS

Rice crispy treats are a perennial party hit with their combination of sweetness and crunchy stickiness. A little canna butter makes them extra festive, and since making them only requires low heat, all of the good stuff comes through.

- ¼ cup of canna butter
- 4 cups mini marshmallows or a 10 oz package of regular marshmallows
- 6 cups of crisp rice cereal
- 13" x 9" pan

DIRECTIONS

Melt the canna butter in a large pan over low heat. Add marshmallows and stir constantly until they melt. Keep stirring for 2 minutes more. Remove from heat.

Add crispy rice cereal. Stir until completely coated.

Butter a 13" x 9" inch pan to avoid sticking. Use a buttered spatula or waxed paper to evenly press the rice crispy mix into the pan. Once cooled, cut into small squares and serve.

cause it is a solid at temperatures below 76°F (24°C) and it has a high saturated fat content. That fat content makes it ideal for binding with cannabinoids.

Clarified Butter and Ghee

Clarifying the butter removes the milk solids and water from the butterfat, leaving purer oil. When butter is placed under medium heat it melts and then begins to foam. Under low heat the butter continues cooking. First the foam disappears. Then the butter begins to crackle as the water boils off. The milk solids fall out of the oil, sinking to the bottom of the pan. The clarified butter turns a deep clear yellow, as only the lactose-free oil is left.

The process is essentially the same for ghee. The difference is that, with ghee, the milk fat is allowed to brown slightly, giving the final product a flavor that is alternately described as "caramel," "butterscotch," or "nutty." A pound of butter yields about ¾ of a pound of ghee. Ghee can be cooked at a higher temperature than butter without burning.

You don't have to make ghee in order to use it. Ghee is available at Indian markets and some other grocery stores. Clarified butter and ghee make excellent cannabinated oils.

GOT CANNA MILK?

Cow's milk is a complex fluid of oils, proteins, sugars, hormones, and enzymes. Whole milk contains about 3.5% butterfat, reduced fat milk contains 2% butterfat, and low-fat milk contains 1% butterfat. Since cannabinoids dissolve in oils and fats, it is best to use regular milk to make cannabinated milk recipes.

Vegans or the lactose intolerant can substitute soy, almond, or coconut milk. Almond milk—at 6g of fat per cup, compared to the 9g of fat in whole milk—will not bind quite as readily with cannabinoids, but it is still higher in fat than 2% dairy milk. Coconut milk, at 3.6 g of fat, falls between 1% and 2% dairy milk. If a non-fat milk or low-fat milk substitute such as rice or soy milk is used some fat should be added to create a more soluble medium. Two teaspoons of oil increases the fat content by 1%. Adding enough oil to increase the fat content to 3%–4% enhances the liquid's extraction properties.

All types of cow's milk and many milk alternatives, such as almond milk, contain the very powerful emulsifier lecithin. The combination of oils that dissolve the cannabinoids and an emulsifier that holds the cannabinoid-rich oil in suspension makes milk an excellent food for ingesting cannabis.

Canna milk can be consumed fresh by itself, used in recipes, or mixed in other beverages, such as tea or coffee. The caffeine in black teas and coffee may hasten the onset of the cannabinoid effects or enhance them. Caffeine increases marijuana's stimulating properties and counterbalances sedating effects.

Indian chai is a great tea for combining with canna milk because it is traditionally made with equal parts of water and milk, and the spices impart a strong but enjoyable flavor that masks the cannabis. Spices include clove, cinnamon, cardamom, and ginger, as well as vanilla bean, black pepper, or anise, and other Indian spices not commonly used in the United States. The exotic spices gently transport you from your everyday world to a soothing tranquility where soon the first waves of highness float into your mind: exquisite.

Coffee's rich, complex flavors make an enjoyable marijuana beverage. WAMM's Mother's Milk makes a knockout café au lait. Finely ground hash can be combined with already-made coffee in a small pan over low heat. Stir for a few minutes until the hash has thoroughly dissolved and is mixed evenly in the drink. Sweeten to taste and serve warm or over ice.

WAMM's Mother's Milk

From Wo/Men's Alliance for Medical Marijuana (WAMM.org)

- 1 oz marijuana leaf that has been crumbled or ground to a fine consistency
- 2 qt whole milk (or almond or coconut milk)

Combine leaf and milk in a Crockpot and cook on low for a minimum of 2 hours. WAMM recommends a cooking time of 8 to 12 hours. Do not open. Do not stir. Do not worry.

The plant material may float; that's fine. Strain the plant material from the mixture using a cheesecloth- or panty hose–lined strainer.

For a little flavor add cinnamon, nutmeg, ginger, or other spices near the end of the cooking process or after milk is finished.

Depending on the potency of the marijuana used, serving sizes may range from ⅛ to ¼ cup.

It will remain fresh in the refrigerator no longer than regular milk, but it can be frozen. One convenient method of storing it is to fill ice-cube trays. Once frozen, store the milk cubes in sealed containers in the freezer to prevent dehydration.

Bhang Lassi

Bhang Lassi is the traditional Indian beverage for Holi, the Hindu celebration of spring, but it is imbibed all year round. A curd-based drink flavored with sugar and spices, it can also be made with yogurt and milk. You can make a Bhang Lassi at home with canna milk or some hash or kief.

In India, Bhang Lassi is prepared by mixing a bhang ball (typically a blend of oily hash and finely ground dried bud) with hot milk that has usually been infused with almond paste, a bit of coconut milk or butter, and some ginger, saffron, or other spices. Vendors, like chefs, have their own recipes using different combinations of spices. This is my recipe. Experiment based on your own taste.

- 1½ cups yogurt/curd, chilled
- ½ cup canna milk
- 4–8 tsp sugar to taste
- ½ tsp cardamom powder (optional)
- 1 pinch saffron (optional)
- 1 pinch garam masala (optional)
- 1 tsp rose water (optional)
- 1 tsp of almond paste, chopped almonds, or pistachios

Mix the ingredients with a blender. Serve over ice.

To make this recipe with hash or kief instead of canna milk, gently heat the ½ cup of milk and mix in the amount of hash or kief desired, stirring constantly for 15 minutes. Do not let it boil. Combine with the other ingredients, and serve over ice.

WATER-BASED CANNA TEA

Marijuana teas are common folk medicines used for upset stomachs of children and adults in Jamaica. Cannabinoids are weakly soluble in hot water, so making a tea by boiling buds, leaf, or trim in water will not extract much of them. The heat and agitation of boiling knocks some of the cannabinoids from the leaves. They float loose in the water. Many of the pigments and terpenes that give marijuana its color and flavor are water soluble, so the tea takes on a pleasing color and aroma and has a mild psychoactive effect. Adding dry lecithin granules, which are emulsifiers, helps the cannabinoids mix into the tea.

MARIJUANA FLOUR

Ground marijuana can be substituted for part of the flour in a recipe. I tasted bread made with whole wheat and hempseed flour with finely ground marijuana. It had a pleasant, savory taste. When used as a replacement for flour, dried marijuana should only be used in a ratio of one part ground leaf material to two parts regular flour to maintain a good texture and taste.

To turn leaf or bud into flour, simply grind it thoroughly in a clean coffee grinder. If the plant material is in pieces too big for a grinder, run it through a food processor or flour mill first. After grinding, use a flour sifter to ensure your marijuana flour has a consistency much like wheat flour.

Preparing marijuana flour with butter, margarine, or oil makes it even more effective and can be used to replace the flour and part of the oil or butter in a recipe. This method converts the THC acid to THC, dissolves some cannabinoids into the butter, and eases digestion.

To Make Potentiated Flour

Melt two cups of butter (four sticks) or oil in a skillet. Reduce marijuana leaf to a flour-like consistency in a blender or coffee grinder. Add 1½ to 2 cups leaf flour to the melted butter, margarine, or oil. Cook covered on lowest heat for 20 minutes. Stir frequently to prevent burning and reduce hot spots that will evaporate the THC and other cannabinoids. Add this flour to any standard recipe that calls for flour and butter or oil, reducing the regular flour and butter by the amount replaced with marijuana buttered flour.

ADDING DIRECTLY TO FOOD

Just as no two cooks make the sauce exactly alike, there are many recipes, methods, and techniques of preparing herb for ingestion. The most popular ones are adding the herb directly to the recipe, dissolving the cannabinoids in butter, oil, or alcohol, or using milk to dissolve and emulsify them.

Although people have tried adding cannabis to everything from soups and salads to meatloaves and lasagnas to desserts, some foods are better for delivering cannabinoids than others. Foods that contain the key ingredients in which cannabinoids dissolve will make the most efficient use of the THC in the plant material. Snacks or bite-sized foods are better than heavy or filling dishes because they do not tax the digestive system.

I was dining at a grower's home. He said to me, "Notice the third shaker on the table?" There were three shakers: salt, pepper, and golden glands—kief. "I use the glands on food all the time," he told me. "At first the grittiness got to me, but now I hardly notice it. It has sort of a nutty taste. When I add it to soups or saucy stuff, it melts after a few minutes and blends in. The glands tend to stick together in the shaker, so I added about 10 grains of uncooked rice. Problem solved."

Marijuana and kief can be added directly to food, just as you would another spice or herb. In fact, in Cambodia low-grade marijuana is for sale in the vegetable market for exactly that purpose. It is added to a dish just like parsley. Either whole sprigs or chopped pieces are used. This works best when the food to which it is added contains some oils or milk fats and undergoes mild or brief heating.

Finely ground trim or fan leaves can be used in soups, stews, sauces, and gravies including curries, molés, and barbecue sauce. The most important consideration when adding this magic spice to your recipe is to figure the number of servings people are likely to eat and to add enough, but not too much. People vary in appetite and tolerance, so it is best to err on the low side, rather than making the food too intense. Some people find raw kief, raw hash, or uncooked plant material difficult to digest. These folks may have a more enjoyable gastronomic experience with cannabinated foods where the cannabis ingredient has been cooked in or the plant material has been strained out.

Some foods have too delicate a taste to absorb the complexity that cannabis lends to food. Many of the pigments and other flavorings can be removed from the cannabis before it is used. Soak the cannabis in room-temperature water for about 15 minutes before using it in the recipe. Strain the leaf from the water. Some of the green flavor and pigments will stay behind in the water, but the leaf will still hold the glands. They are ready to use in recipes.

Ganja Guacamole

Avocados contain 15% or more oil, making them a good food to mix with marijuana.

Medicated guacamole.

Ingredients

- 3 avocados

- 1 tsp oil (or canna oil, for an ultra-potent batch)

- 1½–2 grams of ground marijuana

- 1 lime

- 1 tsp salt

- ½ cup diced onion

- 3 Tbsp chopped fresh cilantro

- 2 tomatoes, diced

- 1 tsp minced garlic

- Cayenne pepper (optional)

Directions

Place the avocados, oil, ground marijuana, and salt in a bowl. Squeeze in the lime. Mash until puree. Mix in diced onion, tomatoes, cilantro, and garlic. Add cayenne pepper to taste for an extra kick. For best results, refrigerate for two hours before serving. Serves 4–6.

FOOD ADVENTURES

As you explore the world of cannabinated food beyond brownies, here is a list of food suggestions:

Photo: Joe Burull

- Flavor extracts, particularly orange extract, seem to neutralize cannabis odors. Just add a teaspoon to any cookie or cake recipe. Orange extract imparts a nice fruity flavor to baked goods and is good with chocolate. Orange extract can also be used when making marijuana butter or oil.

- Strong spices such as ginger, cinnamon, cloves, or nutmeg mask the smell of marijuana when making baked goods. A teaspoon of any of these spices added to cookie recipes blends well with the taste of marijuana leaf. Chocolate also helps neutralize the smell of marijuana and disguises any green coloration.

- Light foods and snacks are the best match when looking for recipes to cannabinate. Yummy foods that make great candidates for cannabinating include the following:

  - Hummus and other dips

  - Banana bread and other dessert breads

  - Chocolate pudding

  - Ginger cookies, peanut butter cookies, or your other favorite cookie recipes

A BIT ABOUT COOKING TIMES

Many edible oil and butter makers think that soaking the cannabis for long periods of time, between 2 to 12 hours, increases the potency or effects. I think that almost all of the cannabinoids and terpenes dissolve soon after they mix with the warm oil, and certainly after an hour. So the recipes here have been modified to reflect that viewpoint. You may wish to experiment with longer cooking times and see what you think.

STORAGE

Cannabinated foods are the same as other marijuana products. Heat, light, and oxygen deplete THC and other cannabinoids over time. Sealed, opaque containers protect your cannabis treats from exposure to oxygen and light. When eggs, milk, butter, or other perishable ingredients have been used the food should be stored in the refrigerator. For longer shelf life, store cannabinated foods in the freezer. Wherever and however you store them, label them clearly with the date they were made and something that makes it obvious that they've got the magic ingredient.

Chapter 12.

Topical Uses of Marijuana

Herbs have been used to treat skin problems for thousands of years. Five thousand years ago, Ayurvedic practitioners used marijuana preparations. Cannabis-enriched lotions, salves, and other topically applied products are still used today. Marijuana's active ingredients—cannabinoids and terpenoid essential oils—are absorbed through the skin for direct therapeutic effect.

Indications include arthritis, inflammation, rheumatism, sore joints and muscles, and to aid the healing of bone fractures. They are also used for a myriad of skin conditions, including burns, eczema, psoriasis, pruritis (itching), abrasions, and sores. Skin cancers have been reduced or eliminated by directly applying concentrated cannabis oil extracts to the tumors in both humans and dogs. Even migraines are treated by applying a marijuana topical to the forehead, temples, and neck.

Cannabis topicals work especially well for localized pain and inflammation. Skin cells have both CB1 and CB2 receptors that cannabinoids act on for therapeutic effect. With pain, the presence of phytocannabinoids directs the firing nerves to reduce their signaling, alleviating the discomfort. People's lives

Lotions made with cannabis penetrate the skin to relieve aches and inflammation. A commercially produced brand is docGreen's Therapeutic Healing Cream. It is gentle yet effective and comes in an assortment of scents.

have been changed using marijuana topicals, including those who have been able to stop taking opiate narcotics for pain, grandparents with severe arthritis who have been able to hold their grandkids for the first time, and musicians who are able to use their fingers again.

When applied topically, cannabinoids are not absorbed in large enough quantities to affect consciousness. In very rare cases, experienced users who are highly sensitive to marijuana's effects say they notice a little something. Absorption through the skin does not appear to produce the same marijuana metabolites as ingesting or inhaling it, so there is little risk of testing positive, even with regular use. That includes marijuana topicals as a potential choice for people whose jobs require drug testing.

Topicals vary in how well they transport the cannabinoids and terpenes, as well as the time they require to do it. The active constituents in marijuana—THC and other cannabinoids and terpenes—absorb more readily and evenly when they are dissolved in a solution. They are lipophilic, meaning that they are soluble in alcohol, fats, and oils.

Cannabinoids' affinity for oils means that they are easily dissolved in lotions and salves that contain alcohol, glycerin, or oils. These help the cannabinoids penetrate the outer layer of skin.

Taking a hot bath or shower, soaking the area to be treated in hot water, or adding heat using a heating pad before applying a topical marijuana product increases how much will be absorbed because the heat opens skin pores. Adding capsaicin (found in hot peppers) is another way to add some heat and open the pores. Be careful—too much capsaicin can create a burning sensation. St. John's Wort or other homeopathic herbs can also be added to the topical to help your skin along with the healing cannabinoids.

Covering an area treated with a cannabis-infused lotion can increase absorption by a factor of ten. Transdermal cannabis patches are now available from some dispensaries, but you can achieve the same effect by simply applying a cannabis topical to the affected area and covering it with a bandage.

Topical preparations that have some alcohol content may be absorbed better because the alcohol opens up skin pores. Applying rubbing alcohol to an area of soreness or inflammation before applying the marijuana topical increases absorption, though alcohol should never be used if the skin is cracked or there are open wounds or sores. Alcohol can create a burning sensation and dries out the skin.

An increasing variety of topical ointments, salves, and other marijuana-infused topical preparations are available in dispensaries. Select products that use the highest quality ingredients, as your skin will absorb the bad as readily as the good. Not all states require complete labeling on cannabis products, so do some research. Stay away from products that contain parabens (used as preservatives) or petroleum-based chemicals (some artificial fragrances), as these can cause a host of other health problems.

Making your own topical is a bit more involved than making canna butter or a tasty batch of magic brownies, but it doesn't have to be. It's simple to make a poultice.

One advantage of making your own medicinal topicals is that you choose the ingredients. Marijuana is not the only medicinal herb that can be used. For instance, if you want a topical to combat inflammation, add to your marijuana topical herbs such as aloe vera, boswellia (frankincense), camphor, eucalyptus, ginger, or mints. Dried calendula flower petals and comfrey are popular, proven herbs that can provide healing benefits. For an analgesic marijuana-infused oil or ointment, adding arnica, willow, balm of gilead (poplar buds), or anything with capsaicin makes it even more soothing. A few drops of Vitamin E enhance its restorative effects on skin.

Shea butter, olive oil, beeswax, and other quality products that can be used as bases for a topical are widely available from local health food stores and on the Internet. Olive oil and shea butter promote absorption, while beeswax is more surface and sealing.

As with all things marijuana, the quality of your final product and its effects is largely determined by the quality of the materials you start with. Many people use nothing but trim and other material that would otherwise be discarded. To produce the finest grade, start with bud. The variety of marijuana used influences its topical effects, because of variation in the cannabinoid and terpene profiles.

MARIJUANA ROOT APPLICATIONS

Marijuana roots have historically had a place in topical preparations, too, with some made exclusively from boiled roots or in combination with stalks. The earliest recorded medicinal use of hemp root is in Chinese medicine from 5,000 years ago, which recommended juicing the root or using it as a paste for pain relief. Ancient Roman medicine employed boiled hemp root to alleviate gout and joint pain and applied raw root on burns. Soaked marijuana root was being used in poultices in Europe by the sixteenth century to relieve gout and arthritis, and fresh juice was reported as good for burns. In Eastern Europe boiled root was a traditional treatment for all types of skin inflammation.

The properties of roots of different varieties may be as variable as the plants that grow from them. The composition of roots has been studied far less than other parts of the plant, but terpenes have been identified such as friedelin, which helps fight pain, inflammation, and fever. Some studies have found alkaloids in varying concentrations, including pyrrolidine and piperidine, as well as choline and atropine, which are also biologically active. Cannabinoids have also been detected in low concentrations.

Boiling is one of the most common ways of preparing marijuana root for topical use, sometimes in combination with oils. When boiled for many hours it produces a dark, oily substance that can be directly applied or used in a poultice. Roots can also be dried and ground to a powder using a clean coffee grinder, then mixed with oils, salves, or butters. Powdered root mixed with alcohol makes a good liniment.

The essential oils and other components of roots can also be extracted with the technique used for creating a cannabis-infused cooking oil. Just place the root in a slow cooker along with your oil of choice and leave it on low for many, many hours, then strain for use. Coconut oil is a good choice for making a root topical, as it will firm up to a paste at room temperature.

POULTICES

Poultices are the simplest topicals to make. They have been used for thousands of years. There are three methods of preparation: with fresh marijuana leaves, with leaves soaked in alcohol, or mixing dried powder with alcohol, glycerin, oil, or water.

India's Ayurvedic medical tradition uses hemp poultices made by boiling the leaves. Sometimes roots are used as well. Boiled poultices are used to treat bacterial skin infections and inflammation, including hemorrhoids. In India, marijuana poultices made from bruised fresh leaves were a common household remedy for conjunctivitis, swollen joints, inflammation of the testes, and other acute inflammatory conditions, sores, and open wounds. Hemp root has also been used traditionally to make poultices.

Pain-relieving topicals range from alcohol-based sprays to relaxing bath salts.

Photo: Making You Better Brands

The most basic poultice method is to crush freshly harvested fan leaves using a mortar and pestle or blender, turning them into a juicy pulp. Spread the crushed leaf paste on the area to be treated. You can roll fresh leaves between your hands to bruise them, which releases the juice and oils. Carboxylated cannabinoids (THCA, CBDA, etc.), still in their acid form in unheated, untreated marijuana leaves, may have different therapeutic properties than the heated, decarboxylated leaves, and are superior for some uses. Use fresh leaf poultices immediately, as they have a very short shelf life unless refrigerated or frozen.

Adding alcohol to fresh marijuana poultices strips cannabinoids and essential oils from the marijuana leaves and opens the pores of the skin. Both increase the absorption of healing chemicals. Making this poultice simply entails soaking raw marijuana fan leaves in alcohol. A mortar and pestle or blender macerates the blend and increases the amount of medicine dissolved in the alcohol. The longer the leaves soak, the better. An alcohol-based marijuana poultice can be stored for weeks or months in the refrigerator. The alcohol helps preserve it. Isopropyl alcohol, which is a poison, can be used since the poultice is for external use. However, using ethyl alcohol or high-proof drinking alcohol prevents accidents.

Dried and cured trim or bud are excellent ingredients. They contain more decarboxylated THC and CBD. Grind to a fine powder, then mix thoroughly with either alcohol, glycerin, oil, or a mix of these ingredients. Alcohol, glycerin, and oil all combine with the oil-based cannabinoids and terpenes to penetrate the skin.

Glycerin or oil dissolve the active ingredients when they are warm. Heat the mixture keeping the temperature below 150°F (66°C) for 20 minutes. Olive and coconut oils and glycerin work well, but you can infuse your favorite massage oil. Don't heat alcohol without taking precautions because its fumes are dangerous to breathe, and they can explode. Alcohol evaporates quickly with a very low heat. **FOR SAFETY: Heat alcohol only over an enclosed electric heater, in a double boiler, or under very low heat in a well-ventilated space or outdoors.**

Cannabinoids and essential oils do not mix with water, but you can make a paste of marijuana powder and water that can be applied to the skin. Add dry lecithin granules to help the oils and water mix.

SALVES AND OILS

You can enhance a salve or massage oil by adding tincture to it. Start with a ratio of about 1:10—that is, one ounce of marijuana extract to ten ounces of topical.

Cooking oils made with marijuana (chapter 11) can be used topically. Use skin-friendly oils such as almond, cocoa butter, coconut, or olive oil. You can make a balm by combining cannabis oil with aloe vera. Add melted beeswax to the mixture. As it cools it helps thicken the salve.

Use dried leaf trim and root to make an infusion by chopping them in a food processor or blender. Soak in a skin-friendly oil for a few weeks, then strain using a fine mesh or cheesecloth or both. To speed up the process, use a blender to mix the ingredients, then apply low heat for at least 20 minutes to an hour, then strain. If using heat, keep the temperature below 150°F (66°C); a double-boiler is a good stove top tool for managing temperature.

Strain the oil, then mix in softened beeswax, coconut oil, or cocoa butter to thicken the mixture to a salve or lotion consistency. Use mild heat to melt and mix the ingredients, but be careful not to overheat beyond 150°F (66°C). Add beeswax sparingly—too much over-hardens the balm. It can be difficult to judge the thickness while heated, so pull a teaspoon of the mixture and pop it in the freezer for two minutes. If it is still liquid or too soft, add more beeswax. Once you've achieved the desired consistency, remove from heat. Continue stirring the mixture as it cools until it gets to about 90°F–100°F (32°C –38°C). Pour into glass containers for storage before it cools completely.

You can make marijuana massage bars that melt as you rub them on your skin by adding beeswax so that it constitutes about 25% of the mix. Before it cools completely, pour it into a baking pan or molds. If you are using a pan, place it in the refrigerator for a couple of hours. Once it's chilled, cut into squares of the desired size. Store the bars in a cool, dark place.

TOPICAL TINCTURES

Tinctures can be used topically. When used for specific local pain or as part of a treatment for skin cancer, highly concentrated tincture is best. Once the tincture is made following the directions in chapter 9, it is ready for topical use. A noncolored and nonflavored alcohol (ethanol) is best for making a tincture for topical use. Glycerin can be used alone for topicals or mixed with aloe, beeswax, alcohol, and water. Place the topical on a bandage. Alcohol can dry the skin, and should not be used on cracked skin or open wounds as it will create an intense burning sensation.

Tinctures that have been reduced to pure, concentrated cannabis oil are used to treat tumors related to skin and other cancers, as popularized by Rick Simpson and others. Cannabinoids have been shown in many preclinical research studies to reduce cancer tumors by selectively cutting off the blood flow to tumors, reprogramming cancerous cells to die off naturally, and stopping the spread to other cells. The cannabis oil can be used as is by applying directly to the skin and massaging in to help it absorb, and then covering with a dressing. Pure cannabis oil can also be combined with other oils, salves, or butters for topical application, but for cancer treatment the advice is generally to use the strongest concentration possible so the cannabinoids can do their tumor-fighting work.

The differences between purified extracts of marijuana, whether tinctures, oils, or waxes, depend more on the marijuana you start with than the method for producing them. Some processes are easier and require less equipment than others, and care must be used with any method that involves combustible solvents. Alcohol is a preferred solvent because it is easy to obtain, relatively safe to work with, and any residual alcohol left in an extract does not pose health risks. Working with butane, naphtha, and other petroleum-based solvents requires more caution, and care must be exercised to ensure that none of the toxic chemicals used remain in the final product. Purging those solvents 100% requires some technical ability and experience.

Rick Simpson Oil

The most famous of the medicinal oil concentrate-making methods is the one popularized by Rick Simpson. This oil has been used to eliminate skin cancers and for other serious medical purposes that have been documented on the Internet. Known as Rick Simpson Oil or Phoenix Tears, the concentrated cannabis oil extract is made with ether, naphtha, or alcohol. His process is simply to wash high-potency cannabis in naphtha three times, filter, then boil off the naphtha in a rice cooker. That leaves an oil concentrate in the bottom of the rice cooker that can be drawn up in a basting syringe or similar device. Naphtha is close to butane in terms of being a highly dangerous petroleum-based solvent (though a little less explosive than butane). It's also dangerous to ingest because it contains benzene and toluene, so oil made with it is only safe if it is 100% purged. Simpson recommends adding some water at the end of the process and boiling it off to help remove impurities, but that may not remove all of them.

Cannabinoids and Terpenes

So far, more than 750 distinct natural chemical components have been identified in the marijuana plant. Any given strain has about 80 bioactives. The most distinctive and important group is terpenophenolic compounds known as cannabinoids, found in cannabis and nearly nowhere else in the botanical world. Marijuana produces more than 100 unique cannabinoids, though most plants have high concentrations of only a few. The cannabinoid profile of any particular plant depends on many factors, including strain, growing environment, maturity of the plant at harvest, and curing and processing technique. Many cannabinoids act as precursors to others. They chemically change into a different cannabinoid as the plant matures or ages post-harvest. For instance, delta-9 tetrahydrocannabinol (THC), the cannabinoid with powerful psychotropic and therapeutic properties, results from the decarboxylation due to aging or heat of tetrahydrocannabinol acid (THCA), a cannabinoid found in live plants that produces little psychoactive effect.

THE ENDOCANNABINOID SYSTEM

One place we find cannabinoids very similar to those that marijuana produces is in our bodies. Most animals, including humans and other vertebrates, produce their own cannabinoids. These endogenous cannabinoids regulate nerve and immune function and many other critical metabolic processes. This is done in part through a unique process called retrograde signaling. The body's endogenous cannabinoids regulate the nerves' signaling output. In the early 1990s, scientists identified a natural human cannabinoid, or endocannabinoid. It was named anandamide, from the Sanskrit word for bliss, and is chemically described as N-arachidonoylethanolamide (AEA). Since then, four other endogenous cannabinoids have been identified: 2-arachidonoylglycerol (2-AG), 2-arachidonyl glyceryl ether (noladin ether), N-arachidonoyl dopamine (NADA), and virodhamine (OAE).

There are two primary receptors that absorb cannabinoids, known as CB1, found mostly in parts of the brain, and CB2, which is distributed throughout the body but is concentrated in the organs and the gut. The location of those receptors, which have as much affinity for plant cannabinoids as the body's own, has revealed much about how marijuana affects us. Three other probable endocannabinoid receptors have been identified—GPR55, GPR119, and GPR18—though much less is known about their function. A possible sixth endocannabinoid, lysophosphatidylinositol (LPI), has an affinity for the GPR55 receptor.

The location of cannabinoid receptors indicates why it is impossible to fatally overdose on marijuana, no matter how hard you try. Alcohol and drugs derived from the poppy plant attach to receptors in the brainstem, which controls your lungs and heart. These central nervous system depressants slow breathing and heartbeat and, with overdoses, can stop both. In contrast, there are no cannabinoid receptors in that part of the brain. Taking a big hit increases your heart rate and affects your blood pressure, but in a more complicated way, perhaps tied to the dilation of blood vessels, which also contributes to that most telltale sign that someone's been toking—bloodshot eyes.

THE PHYTOCANNABINOIDS

Cannabinoids associated with the marijuana plant are now frequently referred to in scientific work as phytocannabinoids to distinguish them from the naturally occurring cannabinoids in humans and animals. The identification of the CB1 and CB2 cannabinoid receptors has led to the discovery that Echinacea and Cacao and possibly other plants contain organic compounds that also attach to these receptors, meaning those chemicals may also be called phytocannabinoids.

As a result of the tremendous genetic variability of the marijuana plant, the cannabinoid profile of different strains varies enormously. Plants classified as industrial hemp, for example, contain very little THC, usually less than 0.3%. At the other end of the spectrum, the selective breeding programs on the U.S. West Coast and in Holland and Spain have developed potent strains with 20% and more THC. Most psychoactive varieties contain high amounts of THC with very small amounts of cannabidiol (CBD) or other cannabinoids.

In terms of cannabinoid profile, there are three basic cultivars or chemotypes of marijuana—a THCA-dominant, a CBDA-dominant, and a heterozygous THCA/CBDA mix. Thanks to generations of selective breeding by growers seeking plants with mind-blowing highs, the vast majority of marijuana today is of the THCA-dominant type. In the past decade or so, however, breeders interested in the recently discovered medicinal effects of CBD have achieved more CBDA-rich varieties.

While CBD has little psychoactive effect, it has many therapeutic properties, and high-CBD extracts have been effective in alleviating seizures in children with intractable seizure disorders such as Dravet Syndrome. Since the interest in the therapeutic properties of CBD emerged, more varieties contain a small amount of it, as well as high THC numbers. Mainly CBD varieties are available, as well as varieties that contain higher concentrations of cannabigerol (CBG), which treats gastrointestinal disorders and glaucoma.

Cannabinoids are detected in all parts of marijuana plants, even the roots, with the highest concentrations in mature buds and the least in seeds. Most cannabinoids start out in the plant as carboxylic acids. Those acids typically convert to nonacid, neutral cannabinoids after harvest—either by exposure to light and heat in storage or by heating for consumption via cooking, burning, or vaporizing.

The primary cannabinoids are delta-9 THC, CBD, and CBG. Minor cannabinoids include delta-8 THC, CBC, CBE, CBL, CBN, and CBT. Each of these types has several subclasses. For instance, there are at least five CBC-type, eight CBD-type, and 16 CBG-type cannabinoids that differ in appearance and effect because of slightly different side-chain molecular structures. THC also has several subclasses with varying levels of psychoactivity. Nine THC-type cannabinoids have been identified, with the differences being side chains of 1, 3, 4, or 5 carbon atoms. They are THC, THCA-A, THCA-B, THCA-C$_4$, THC-C$_4$, THCVA, THCV, THCA-C$_1$, and THC-C$_1$. Other cannabinoids result from the degradation of these cannabinoids. CBN, for example, results from the degradation of THC, and CBND from the degradation of CBD.

Delta-9 THC (delta-9 tetrahydrocannibinol) is modern marijuana's most common cannabinoid and is by far its most psychoactive component. It accounts for most of the high and much of the plant's therapeutic properties, though phytochemicals in marijuana known as terpenes modify its effects. THC is primarily responsible for appetite stimulation and has been shown to have anti-inflammatory, anti-nausea, pain-relieving, tumor-fighting, and many other therapeutic effects. Actually, THC is found in nine variations with slight differences in their chemical structure. Four or five of these variants have similar effects to THC. For instance, THCV (tetrahydrocannabivarin) is a variant of THC found in some varieties of Asian and African strains that seems to be much faster in onset and quicker to dissipate than standard THC. Even though THCV's psychoactivity appears to be somewhat less than that of THC, it is usually associated with extremely potent weed. THCV also has analgesic, anti-inflammatory, and anticonvulsant effects. Most marijuana has only small amounts of THCV, though varieties have been reported that are 16% THCV.

All THC starts out in fresh plant material as THC acid, or THCA, which is THC with a COOH molecule attached. THCA has no psychotropic effects, but it has many medical uses, and has demonstrated positive effects on the immune system. Applying heat to THCA by smoking or processing plant material removes the COOH molecule in a process called decarboxylation and transforms it into potently psychoactive THC.

THC occurs in all varieties of cannabis, from sinsemilla to industrial hemp, in concentrations that vary from trace amounts to almost all of the cannabinoids present.

Delta-8 THC (delta-8 tetrahydrocannabinol) has some of the same effects as delta-9 THC, such as appetite stimulation, but it is considerably less psychoactive. It results from the decarboxylation of delta-8 THC acid and has no known subtypes.

CBD (cannabidiol) has at least eight subtypes and occurs in almost all cannabis varieties, in quantities that range from trace amounts to almost all of the cannabinoids present. Most THC-rich varieties have little CBD present, while CBD is the primary cannabinoid in most fiber hemp. CBD is not psychoactive in the same manner as THC, but it can be mood-altering and modulate the high produced by THC.

CBD appears to heighten marijuana's sedative effects and to moderate the euphoric effects. It may also delay the onset of the high, but make it last longer. Terms such as "sleepy," "dreamlike," and "contemplative" are often used to describe the effect of marijuana with sizeable proportions of CBD.

CBD has many of the same therapeutic effects as THC, but it appears to achieve them through different biological mechanisms. CBD does not attach as readily to cannabinoid receptors as THC, but it interacts with both CB1 and CB2 receptors in ways that produce its own effects and alter how THC is absorbed. CBD has a marked affinity for serotonin receptors, which are associated with psychological well-being and may account for some of its antipsychotic, anti-anxiety, and hypnotic properties. CBD is also a powerful anti-inflammatory and analgesic, perhaps because it enhances the action of adenosine receptors, which have a role in the management of pain and inflammation. In addition, CBD has antioxidant and neuroprotective properties.

In 2001, GW Pharmaceuticals found that a balanced combination of equal parts CBD and THC offered the best analgesic effects for multiple sclerosis patients. Taken alone, neither CBD nor THC was as effective in treating chronic pain as they were in combination. CBD may also be effective in reducing intraocular pressure, the medical application for glaucoma patients.

In the past few years, CBD has gotten considerable attention for its anticonvulsant properties. Concentrated CBD extracts alleviated the seizures of several children with severe seizure disorders that did not respond to other medications. GW Pharmaceuticals is now testing a CBD extract in clinical trials with children who suffer from intractable seizure conditions.

Plants that have been bred to have high concentrations of THC typically have considerably less CBD. The therapeutic qualities of CBD have also gained the attention of breeders, and more CBD-rich varieties of marijuana are becoming available.

CBG (cannabigerol) is a nonpsychoactive cannabinoid with at least 16 subtypes that is the direct precursor to delta-9 THC, CBD, and CBC. There is rarely much CBG present in mature marijuana, although some varieties have percentages as high as 4%. CBG is an antimicrobial, as are other cannabinoids, and has several other biological effects with therapeutic potential. It is a more powerful pain-killer than THC and may be effective for psoriasis and depression.

CBC (cannabichromine), which results from decarboxylating cannabichromenic acid (CBCA), is inactive in its pure form, but is suspected of potentiating THC. Some tests made for CBD may actually measure CBC, which is chemically similar. CBC is abundant in immature plants and has at least eight subtypes. As with other cannabinoids, varieties have been selectively bred that have substantial concentrations of CBC, and significant amounts have been found in some potent varieties.

CBE (cannabielsoin) is a derivative of CBD that may be found in hash as the result of oxidation or heat. It is also a metabolite of CBD that can be detected in humans.

CBT (cannabitriol) has been found in male flowers, some Asian varieties of cannabis, and occasionally in hash.

CBN (cannabinol) is produced by the degradation of THC after harvest. It is only slightly psychoactive, at best about 10% of THC's effect. Fresh samples of marijuana contain very little CBN, but curing, poor storage, or processing can cause the THC content to be oxidized into CBN. When marijuana is pressed for shipping, the resin glands that hold and protect THC are sometimes ruptured, exposing the cannabinoids to air and increasing the rate of oxidation.

CBN seems to exaggerate THC's disorienting qualities, making you feel more drugged, dizzy, or generally untogether, but not necessarily higher. With a significant proportion of CBN, the high may start well and then feel as if it never reaches its peak, and may not last long.

How to Read the Following Charts

Reading horizontally: The physical state of cannabis is raw, heated, aged. Raw refers to the fresh plant. Aged refers to the degradation effects of UV-light, oxidation, and isomerization.

Reading vertically: How do cannabinoids relate to each other? Where do they come from?

Courtesy of Elemental Wellness Medical Cannabis Dispensary

UNDERSTANDING MEDICAL CANNABIS
Cannabinoids and Their Relationships

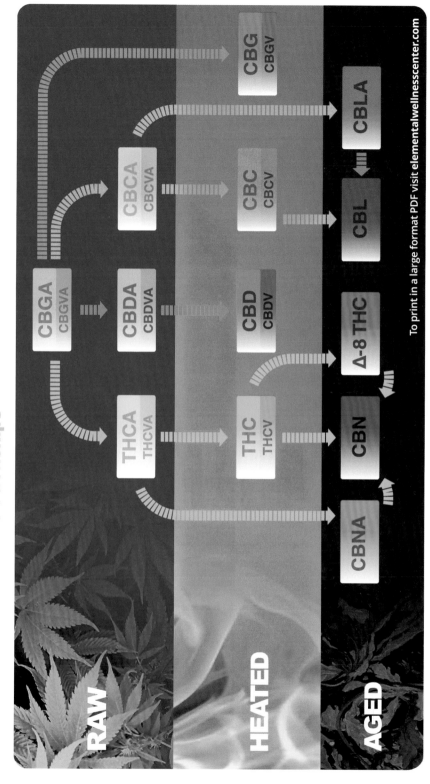

Courtesy of Elemental Wellness Medical Cannabis Dispensary

To print in a large format PDF visit elementalwellnesscenter.com

Cannabinoids and Their Therapeutic Effects

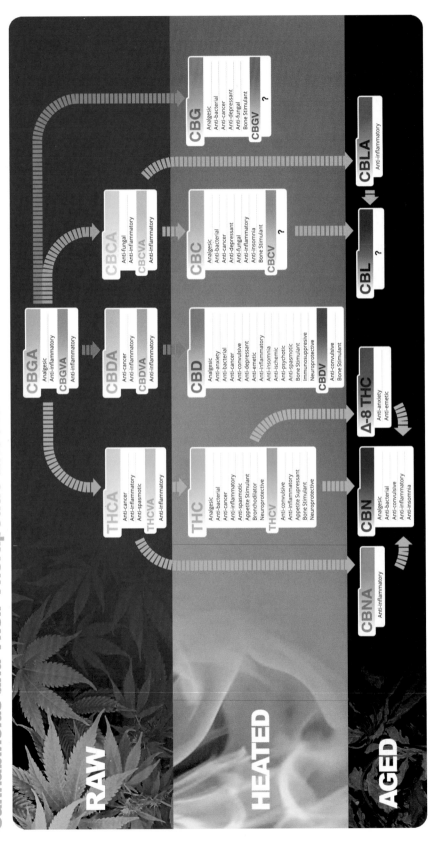

Courtesy of Elemental Wellness Medical Cannabis Dispensary

Cannabinoids, Therapeutic Effects and Synergistic Terpenoids

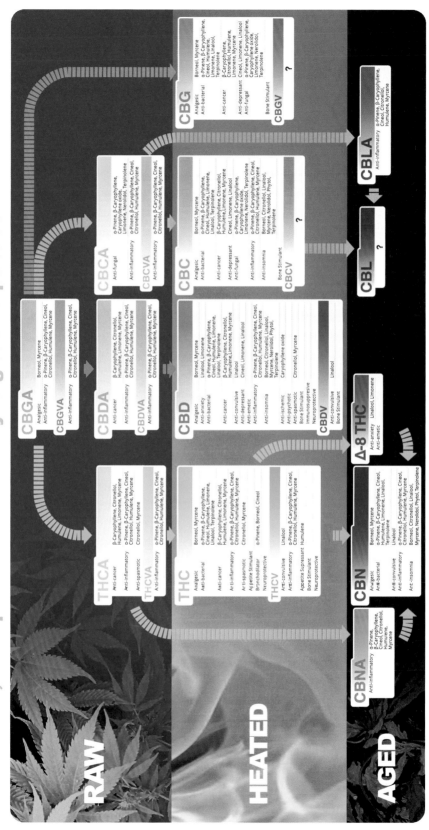

Courtesy of Elemental Wellness Medical Cannabis Dispensary

THE TERPENES

Like many other plants, cannabis contains terpenes and flavonoids. Terpenes impart the strong odors characteristic of good weed and have therapeutic properties of their own. Terpenes also interact with cannabinoids in ways that affect how the body absorbs and utilizes them.

Terpenes are essential oils that plants produce for one of three reasons: to attract pollinators, to attract predators of herbivores that attack them, and to repel and/or kill predators and pathogens. Each terpene has a characteristic odor easily recognizable for its association with other plants. The recipe of terpenes and their concentration varies by variety. The combination gives marijuana strains identifiable odors: sour, diesel, fruity, pine, etc. The amount of any given terpene in the marijuana you smoke or ingest is relatively small—usually no more than a fraction of a percent.

Since the bioavailability of terpenes is in the range of 18%, roughly similar to THC and other cannabinoids, only tiny amounts of terpenes make it into the bloodstream. Still they have a tremendous medical and psychoactive effect.

Terpenes are used in aromatherapy to alter mood, attitude, and outlook, as well as for physical effects. When used in conjunction with cannabis they influence the high. Most experienced marijuana consumers understand this informally. If you were to be handed a bud, your first action would probably be to look at it. The second thing you would do is smell it. THC, CBD, and the other cannabinoids have no odor. What you would be smelling are the terpenes. You know from experience that the odor of the bud is an indication of the kind of high it produces. That's why two different varieties that have the same THC content can have different effects—it's the terpenes.

The same terpenes found in marijuana appear in different types of plants. For instance, a bud with a citrus odor such as lemon or grapefruit most likely has limonene, which is associated with those fruits. Other fruit and flower odors are often produced from other familiar terpenes, such as pinene, which has a pine-like odor, and myrcene, which has a faint nutty odor, to name just a few of many. You could say THC is the engine that drives the high, and the terpenes are the steering wheel. Is it taking you up? Is it focusing, relaxing, or making you tired or energetic? It's the terpenes.

It takes only a few parts per million (ppm) of most terpenes for you to smell and identify the scent. Even at these low levels they have a profound effect on us psychically, psychologically, physiologically, and medically. Many of the effects of terpenes derive from the activation of the olfactory bulb, the part of your brain that processes odor. The nose odor receptors are sensors with their own direct connection to the brain and are used to process information about the environment. This is why aromas have such a powerful effect. That smile your friends get when you stick some fine bud under their noses and let them take a big sniff isn't just anticipation of the experience that's coming; the smell is having its own effect.

Some terpenes, such as myrcene, have an effect once they enter the bloodstream. Myrcene passes through the blood-brain barrier and increases its porosity so that more THC enters faster, causing a quick-onset high. B-caryophyllene is associated with a relaxed feeling and sociability. Other terpenes have other special effects. Terpenes may have more effect on the high and some medical conditions than CBD or cannabinoids other than THC.

To fully experience the power of terpenes, use a vaporizer. The essence you smell and taste is mostly terpenes and flavonoids. Heavy smoke from combusting plant material can be satisfying, but the tars and smoke mask the delicate odors. Terpenes have a range of temperatures at which they begin to evaporate, just like cannabinoids. Some are volatile at 70°F (21°C). Most of them evaporate at below 150°F (66°C). So vaporizing releases the cannabinoids and virtually all of the terpenes and flavonoids.

As cannabis consumers become connoisseurs and changing laws make more choices available, terpene profiles will gain importance. When confronted by a dozen or more strains at a dispensary, all of which are of superior quality and pack substantial percentages of THC and possibly CBD, the terpene profiles of particular strains will make them more popular than others. Actually, that already happens. Odors signal the quality of the bud. The delineation of terpenes that is happening now will help consumers choose the variety that is right for them.

The cannabinoids and terpenes are produced in the trichomes that are most abundant around the maturing female flowers. The oil the glands hold has a mixture of cannabinoids and terpenes.

Two of the most important terpenes in terms of their effects are β-myrcene and Linalool.

β-myrcene is the most abundant terpene in most varieties. It has anti-inflammatory, analgesic, antibiotic, and antimutagenic properties. It is found in Cavicol and other varieties of mangoes.

Linalool is also found in lavender, roses, and some citrus. It is typically only about 5% of the essential oils in marijuana, but it has important biological effects. Linalool is the most powerful sedative of all the terpenes. It is antidepressant and helps reduce anxiety.

α-**terpinol** is a sedative and acts synergistically with linalool to enhance the effect. It is antidepressant and helps reduce anxiety.

d-limonene is found in abundance in citrus. It is focusing, stimulating, antidepressant, and helps reduce anxiety.

a-terpineol has antibiotic, antioxidant, and antimalarial properties. It has a vaporizing temperature of more than 426°F (219°C), notably higher than some cannabinoids and other terpenes.

ß-caryophyllene lightens people's moods and helps them socialize. It has anti-inflammatory, antimalarial, and cytoprotective properties. It vaporizes at 246°F (119°C).

Pulegone has sedative and other properties.

1,8-cineole (eucalyptol) has stimulant, antibiotic, antiviral, and anti-inflammatory properties.

a-pinene has a pine-like odor and has anti-inflammatory, antibiotic, stimulant, and other properties.

p-cymene is an antibiotic.

Appendix 2.

Equivalents and Conversions

Measurement Abbreviations

t	=	teaspoon
g	=	gram
T	=	tablespoon
kg	=	kilogram
c	=	cup
mL	=	milliliter
pt	=	pint
L	=	liter
qt	=	quart
oz	=	ounce
lb	=	pound

Fluid Equivalents

3 t	=	1 T	=	14.68 mL
4 T	=	¹⁄₄ c	=	59.1 mL
1 c	=	8 oz	=	236 mL
2 c	=	1 pt	=	473 mL
2 pt	=	1 qt	=	0.94 L

Dry Equivalents

¹⁄₄ oz	=	7.1 g		
¹⁄₂ oz	=	14.2 g		
1 oz	=	28.4 g		
8 oz	=	227 g		
16 oz	=	454 g	=	1 lb
1000 g	=	1 kg	=	2.2 lb
100 kg	=	a federal rap		

U.S. Food Measures

Butter:	1 lb	=	2 c
Flour:	1 lb	=	4 c
Sugar:	1 lb	=	2 c

Temperature Conversions

Fahrenheit	Celsius
150	66
212	100
250	121
275	135
300	149
325	163
350	177
375	191
400	204
425	218
450	232
475	246
500	260
550	288
600	316

Powdered Marijuana Leaf and Bud

1 t	=	1.8 g		
1 T	=	5.5 g	=	~$^1/_4$ oz
$^1/_4$ c	=	22.4 g		
$^1/_3$ c	=	28 g	=	1 oz
$^1/_2$ c	=	45 g		
$^2/_3$ c	=	56 g	=	2 oz
1 c	=	84 g	=	3 oz

Screen Sizes

100 microns = 0.1 millimeter = 0.0039 inches

75–125 micron screen = approximately 100–150 strands per inch screen

Typical marijuana gland size range: 75–125 microns

Appendix 3.

Glossary

710: the cannabis oil community's version of "420"; "oil" upside down

absolute: the dewaxed essence of a botanical extraction

boiling point: the temperature at which a substance turns to gas; cannabinoids and terpenes have different temperatures at which the oils vaporize and escape into the air

botanical extraction: the process of removing a plant's essential oils, resins, or other components through any number of means (mechanical, steam, solvent, etc.)

butane: simple, explosive hydrocarbon used in botanical extractions

BHO: abbreviation for "butane hash oil"; can refer to any number of concentrates derived from butane extraction; also can refer to raw, unpurged, liquid solution of butane and extract

bubble hash: cannabis glands concentrated by means of ice water

budder: a type of BHO that is opaque and malleable

buddering: when translucent BHO clouds over

bulbous trichome: the smallest of the marijuana plant's cannabinoid-rich glands, measuring from 15 to 30 micrometers; the "foot" and "stalk" are one to four cells, as is the "head" of the gland

cannabidiol: second most common cannabinoid found in cannabis, with many confirmed therapeutic benefits

cannabinoid: a class of molecules produced by cannabis; there are more than 100 of them. Many interact with the human nervous system to produce the wide variety of cannabis's effects.

capitate-sessile trichome: cannabinoid-rich marijuana glands, measuring from 25 to 100 micrometers, that stay close to the plant surface on stalks a cell or two high

capitate-stalked trichome: the largest and most abundant of the cannabinoid-rich marijuana glands, measuring from 150 to 500 micrometers; contains the bulk of the cannabinoids and terpenes

concrete: a botanical extraction that includes the plant's essential oils, as well as its waxes and lipids

conduction: heat transfer through solid matter, such as metal; a conduction vaporizer has a metal or other hot element as its heat source

convection: the transfer of heat by automatic circulation of a fluid; a convection vaporizer circulates hot air or fluid to produce the proper temperature

critical phase: a fourth phase of matter; a combination of intense pressure and/or temperature. Critical CO_2 has a different solubility than liquid or gas.

critical point: the combination of temperature and pressure beyond which a substance is in its critical range. Supercritical substances have different solubility than their other phases, opening the door for extraction.

dab: a small amount of concentrated marijuana extract (i.e., BHO), equivalent in size to a grain of white rice

dab rig (oil rig): a water filtration pipe designed for vaporizing concentrates

decarboxylation: the removal of a carboxyl, which is a carbonate molecule (COOH). When carboxyl molecules are attached to the THC molecule, it is called THCA, or THC acid. In this form, THC lacks most of its psychoactivity. Decarboxylation removes the COOH acid molecule, leaving behind THC. Mild heat is often used to convert THCA to THC. This happens during drying, vaporization, and smoking. Some decarboxylation happens naturally as marijuana cures and ages.

diffusivity: the ability of a substance to dissolve into another substance, a factor in CO_2 extraction

dry sift: another term for kief

endocannabinoid: the natural cannabinoids produced in the body by humans and other vertebrate animals that regulate complex biological processes, including those of the immune system; endocannabinoids attach to specific receptors that also respond to phytocannabinoids

essential oil: a concentrated hydrophobic liquid containing volatile aroma compounds from plants

emulsifiers: Emulsifiers promote suspension of small, fatty globules in water. When water and oil are mixed together, they quickly separate. However, in the presence of an emulsifier the oil breaks into small bits suspended in the water. Two examples of this are milk and commercial salad dressings. Lecithin is a common emulsifier that is available in health food stores.

gland: the trichome filled with cannabinoids and other essential oils, found on external surfaces of the plant, especially the upper side of leaves surrounding the female flowers

health stone: a porous ceramic filter placed in a pipe bowl used to smoke concentrates

hydrophobic: resistant to water—for instance, the waxy covering of trichomes; chemically, substances that don't combine with water

inflorescence: the botanical term for marijuana buds or flowers, referring to a cluster of flowers on a stem composed of a main branch or arrangement of branches

juicing: the process of reducing to a liquid the nutrients and other ingredients of fresh plant material either by pressing or blending

leaf: in the context of this book, the term is used to denote fan or large sun leaves, as well as the larger secondary leaves of the cannabis plant

lipid: a class of naturally occurring hydrophobic or amphiphilic small molecules that includes fats and waxes; they are present in cannabis

loupe: a small magnifying glass utilized by photographers; can be used to observe plant surfaces—an 8X loupe is sufficient for this purpose. Inexpensive 30X plastic scopes are available in toy stores.

mixture: a suspension of (an) insoluble compound(s), such as oil in water—milk and gravy are examples

nail: a small, titanium or quartz platform for vaporizing concentrates; comes with or without a dome

naphtha: a class of petroleum-based solvents that can be used to extract cannabis oil

nucleation: the gathering of fats in a raw BHO slab, leading to buddering

oil: a catch-all term that refers to any number of concentrates of different consistencies, as well as raw, unpurged BHO or CO_2 extract

oxidation: the action of oxygen when it unites with another substance chemically. This happens quickly in fire, but also takes place at a much slower pace at room temperature. For marijuana and its products, oxidation is deterioration. The oxygen in air interacts with marijuana to reduce its THC content.

phase: the state of matter, usually in one of three states: solid, liquid, and gas; supercritical is a fourth state created under unusual conditions

phytocannabinoids: the cannabinoids produced by plants, as distinguished from endocannabinoids, the ones produced naturally by humans and animals

psi: pounds per square inch, a measure of pressure in extraction

polarity: the type and strength of a molecule's electric charge; polarity affects solubility

poultice: a mollifying remedy of a moist nature applied to skin inflammations; poultice ingredients include minerals, herbs, or other medicinals

ppm: parts per million; used here as a measure of residual solvent in an extract

purge: the act of removing a solvent from a solution, as occurs during BHO or CO_2 extraction

pyrolytic compounds: compounds produced by chemical changes brought about by the action of heat in the absence of oxygen. These compounds often consist of carcinogenic hydrocarbons, often gasses.

self-titrate: to determine one's dosage for oneself

sinsemilla: the name given to the seedless buds harvested from an unfertilized female marijuana plant. Because the flowers were not pollinated, the plant puts more energy into producing flowers, which increases the yield. Sinsemilla is often used to generically refer to potent marijuana.

shatter: a highly regarded type of BHO characterized by its translucence and its brittleness at room temperature

skillet/swing: a type of heating element used in dabbing concentrates

solution: when a substance dissolves, its molecules actually form a loose molecular relationship with the liquid that it dissolves into. For instance, sugar in hot water or chlorine in a pool are solutions—their molecules spread out so that they are evenly spaced throughout the liquid.

solubility: the property of a solid, liquid, or gaseous chemical solute that allows it to dissolve in a solid, liquid, or gaseous solvent to form a homogeneous solution of the solute in the solvent

solvent: a substance that dissolves another substance, creating a solution—water is the most basic solvent in the universe; because cannabinoids and terpenes are oils, solvents used to extract them include alcohol, petroleum-based liquids, and liquid CO_2

strain: a type of marijuana determined by its genes, which affect extraction output and its effects

subcritical: CO_2 extraction done below the critical temperature and pressure point of carbon dioxide when it turns to liquid

sublingual: a method of using tinctures. The liquid is placed and held under the tongue and is absorbed by the porous mucous membranes lining the mouth and throat. When consumed in this way, absorption is faster than eating because it does not pass through the digestive system before entering the bloodstream, but is slower than smoking. This is a good way to use marijuana for the treatment of nausea without inhaling.

supercritical: an unusual phase that occurs when a substance is held at or pushed past its critical point when it changes from gas to liquid or similar. A supercritical substance has different characteristics (solubility, diffusivity) than the same substance has as a liquid or a gas; it is considered a "cloud."

terpene: the volatile aromatic molecules present in plants including cannabis. They are based on a C^5H^8 model. They are used in aromatherapy and can affect both mood and physical condition.

THC: delta-9 tetrahydrocannabinol, the main psychoactive ingredient in marijuana, present in the plant's external glands, the trichomes

titration: the process of determining the proper dosage for a desired effect

torch: a butane-powered lighter used to rapidly heat nails and skillets

trichome: a three- or four-celled gland with a bulbous head that stretches as it fills with THC and other cannabinoids created in the bulb along the membrane

trim: consists of the small leaves that surround and protect the buds—aside from the buds themselves, the trim has the most concentrated cannabinoid content

vape: to vaporize and inhale marijuana or concentrates

vaporization: the act of gently heating cannabis or concentrates to about 380°F (193°C), at which point the THC turns into a gas and can be inhaled without the carcinogens associated with burning the plant

vape pen: a pen-sized microvaporizer, usually for BHO

wax: a type of BHO; also a substance excreted by cannabis plants to protect themselves from desiccation

winterization: in bio-industry, the act of removing waxes from an oil, usually through the application of cold temperature

Appendix 4.

References

In addition to reports from vaporizer reviewers and interviews with concentrators, extractors, vaporizer inventors, tincture makers, cannabis chefs, water hash bag manufacturers, kiefers, hash pressers, and other cannabis-creative folks, the following books, articles, studies, and websites served as sources for this book. Entries are listed in alphabetical order by title.

Aunt Sandy's Medical Marijuana Cookbook, by Sandy Moriarty. Piedmont, CA: Quick American Publishing, 2010.

Cannabis and Cannabinoids: Pharmacology, Toxicology, and Therapeutic Potential, edited by Franjo Grotenhermen, MD, and Ethan Russo, MD. Binghamton, NY: Hayworth Integrative Healing Press, 2002.

The Cannabis Cookbook: Over 35 Tasty Recipes for Meals, Munchies, and More, by Tom Pilcher. Philadelphia: PA: Running Press, 2007.

The Cannabis Gourmet Cookbook, by Cheri Sicard. Long Beach, CA: Z-Dog Media, 2012.

"Cannabis Vaporizer Combines Efficient Delivery of THC with Effective Suppression of Pyrolytic Compounds," by Dale Gieringer, Scott Goodrich, and Joseph St. Laurent. *Journal of Cannabis Therapeutics* 4 (1), 2004.

"Chemistry and Analysis of Phytocannabinoids and Other Cannabis Constituents," by Rudolf Benneisen. In *Forensic Science and Medicine: Marijuana and the Cannabinoids*, edited by M. A. ElSohly. Totowa: NJ: Humana Press, 2007.

"Decreased Respiratory Symptoms in Cannabis Users Who Vaporize," by Mitch Earleywine and Sara Smucker Barnwell. *Harm Reduction Journal*, 2007.

"The Diverse CB1 and CB2 Receptor Pharmacology of Three Plant Cannabinoids: Δ9-Tetrahydrocannabinol, Cannabidiol and Δ9-Tetrahydrocannabivarin," by R. G. Pertwee. *British Journal of Pharmacology* 153 (2): 199–215, January 2008.

Handbook of Essential Oils: Science, Technology, and Applications, edited by K. Husnu Can Baser and Gerhard Buchbauer. Boca Raton, FL: CRC Press, 2009.

Hashish, by Robert Connell Clarke. Los Angeles, CA: Red Eye Press, 1998.

"Hash Oil Explosions Increasing Across U.S.," *The InfoGram*, February 7, 2013. The U.S. Fire Administration—Emergency Management and Response—Information Sharing and Analysis Center (EMR-ISAC).

Marijuana: Gateway to Health, by Clint Werner. San Francisco, CA: Dachstar Press, 2011.

Marijuana Herbal Cookbook, by Tom Flowers. CA: Flowers Publishing, 1995.

The Science of Marijuana, by Leslie L. Iversen. Oxford, UK: Oxford University Press, 2000.

"Seasonal Fluctuations in Cannabinoid Content of Kansas Marijuana," by R. P. Latta and B. J. Eaton. *Economic Botany* 29: 153–163, April–June 1975.

"Standards of Identity, Analysis, and Quality Control," edited by Roy Upton, et al. *Cannabis Inflorescence: Cannabis* Spp. American Herbal Pharmacopoeia, 2013.

Stir Crazy: Cooking with Cannabis, by Bobcat Press. Oakland, CA: Quick American Archives, 1999.

A Treasury of Hashish, by Dr. Alexander Sumach. Toronto, ONT: Stoneworks Publishing Company, 1976.

"Vaporization of Cannabinoids: A Preferable Drug Delivery Route," by Tod. H. Mikuriya, MD. *Schaffer Library of Drug Policy*, 1993.

MORE STUDIES

CDC Safety Guidelines for Butane
http://www.cdc.gov/niosh/docs/81-123/pdfs/0068.pdf

EPA Butane Exposure Guidelines
http://www.epa.gov/oppt/aegl/pubs/butane_interim_dec_2008_v1.pdf

National Institutes of Health Toxicology Data Network (Butane)
TOXNET.nlm.nih.gov

Praxair Material Safety Data Sheet—Butane
http://www.praxair.com/~/media/North%20America/US/Documents/SDS/Butane%20C4H10%20Safety%20Data%20Sheet%20SDS%20P4572.ashx

Additional Information

Matt Rize: Ice Water Extractivist
MattRize.wordpress.com

Rick Simpson's Phoenix Tears (cannabis oil extract)
PhoenixTears.ca

Skunk Pharm Research
SkunkPharmResearch.com

Apeks Supercritical
ApeksSupercritical.com

Bhogart (BHO extractor manufacturer)
Bhogart.com

Eden Labs (SFE machine manufacturer)
EdenLabs.com

Harborside Health Center (concentrate expertise)
HarborsideHealthCenter.com

Oaksterdam University
OaksterdamUniversity.com

Steep Hill Halent: Cannabis Testing Laboratory
SteepHillLab.com

Waters (SFE Systems)
Waters.com

Wildflower seed in the sand and wind
May the four winds blow you home again
Roll away the dew.

INDEX

SPONSORS

We would like to thank the following sponsors, whose support and participation helped make this book possible.

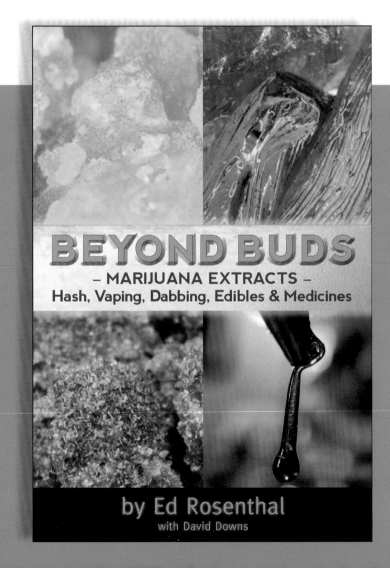

BEYOND BUDS
– MARIJUANA EXTRACTS –
Hash, Vaping, Dabbing, Edibles & Medicines

by Ed Rosenthal
with David Downs

 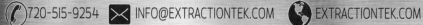

minivapes.co

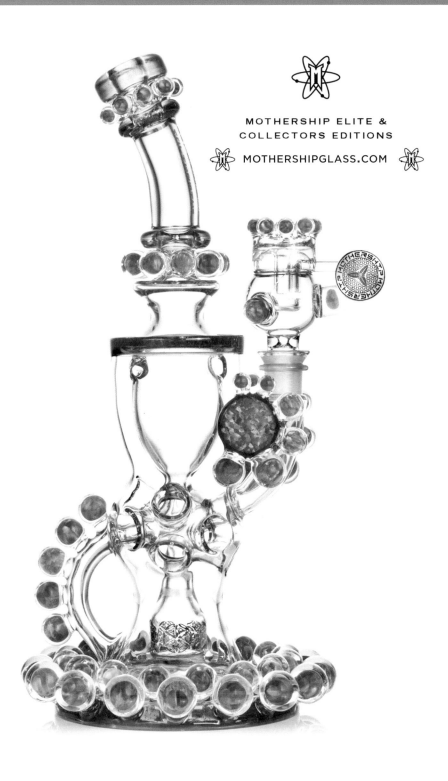

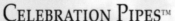

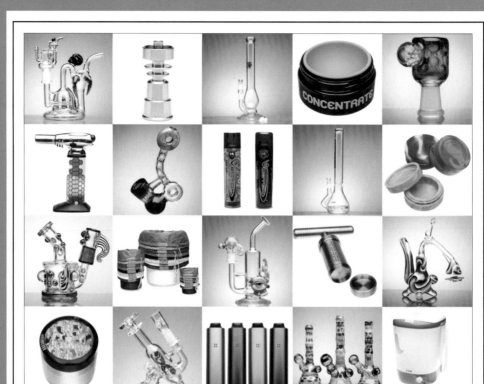

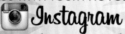

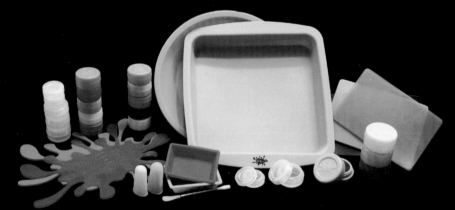

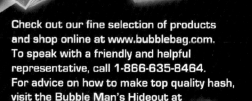

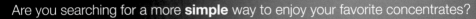

TrimBin ™

High walls keep your work contained and make cleanup easy.

150 micron stainless screen produces only fine-grained, high-grade pollen.

Ergonomic design reduces back, shoulder and wrist fatigue.

Easily collect pollen with the static brush and mirror-finish collection tray.

Increases productivity by alleviating user fatigue and discomfort.

Turn any chair into a comfortable workstation!

Made in California.

HarvestMore ®

harvest-more.com

PINK BELLY extracts

TOP SHELF EXTRACTIONS + BOUTIQUE FLOWERS FROM THE HEART OF SOUTHERN OREGON

FOLLOW US ON INSTAGRAM @PINKBELLYEXTRACTS

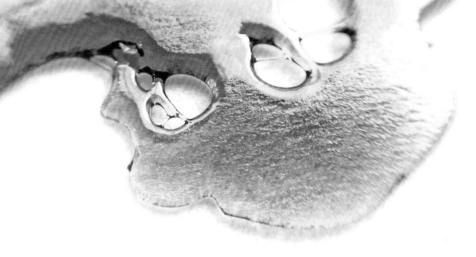

Winterize Your Sesh

Clean extracts are made with the right finesse. Elicit Labs produces winterized absolutes and strives to make cleaner, more potent medicine.

Join the conversation #WINTERIZEYOURSESH

kali
CAPS & CREMES

NONE OF THE FLAVOR ALL OF THE BENEFITS

One of the kindest ways to take your medicine.

• All Natural • 100% Vegetarian • Lab Tested •